SATHER CLASSICAL LECTURES

Volume Fifty-Eight

Fiction as History

Fiction as History

Nero to Julian

G. W. Bowersock

University of California Press

BERKELEY · LOS ANGELES · LONDON

University of California Press
Berkeley and Los Angeles, California

University of California Press, Ltd.
London, England

©1994 by
The Regents of the University of California

Library of Congress Cataloging-in-Publication Data

Bowersock, G. W. (Glen Warren), 1936–
    Fiction as history : Nero to Julian / G. W. Bowersock.
        p.   cm. — (Sather classical lectures ; v. 58)
    Includes bibliographical references (p.   ) and index.
    ISBN 0-520-08824-7
    1. Latin literature—History and criticism.   2. Literature and
history—Rome.   3. Rome—Historiography.   4. Rome—In
literature.
    I. Title   II. Series.
PA6019.B68   1995
870.9'001—dc20   93-49581
                                                                          CIP

9 8 7 6 5 4 3 2 1

"Your story is extremely interesting, Professor, but it differs completely from the accounts in the gospels."

"But surely," replied the professor with a condescending smile, "you of all people must realize that absolutely nothing written in the gospels actually happened. . . ."

"I agree . . . , but I'm afraid that no one is in a position to prove the authenticity of your version either."

"Oh, yes! I can easily confirm it!" rejoined the professor. . . . "The fact is"—here the professor glanced round nervously and dropped his voice to a whisper—"I was there myself."

—M. Bulgakov, *The Master and Margarita*
(translation by M. Glenny)

Contents

Preface

The pages that follow constitute, with the addition of two appendixes, the revised and documented text of the six lectures that I had the honor of delivering as Sather Professor in the Department of Classics at the University of California, Berkeley, in the autumn of 1991. The term I spent at that great university was memorable for me in many ways, but perhaps above all for the hospitality and liveliness of the intellectual community that welcomed me there. I shall always feel an immense debt of gratitude to Mark Griffith, chairman of the department, and to his colleagues, as well as to the remarkably gifted students who participated in my seminar on Roman Syria.

Although my seminar was on a strictly historical subject, I tried to remember in delivering my Sather Lectures that the title of the chair is, in fact, Sather Professor of Classical Literature. I share very much the opinion of Keith Hopkins in a recent article: "Serious historians of the ancient world have often undervalued fiction, if only . . . because by convention history is concerned principally with the recovery of truth about the past. But for social history—for the history of culture, for the history of people's understanding of their own society—fiction occupies a privileged position" (*Past and Present* 138 [1993], 6).

I am conscious of two important predecessors who, in their own Sather Lectures, have touched on the themes I develop here. One was the inimitable Eric Dodds, whose *Greeks and the Irrational* first persuaded classical scholars that dreams, among other shadowy phenomena, deserved serious thought. The other was a pioneer in the study of ancient fiction, Ben Perry, who lectured in 1951 on *The Ancient Romances,* although his book on this subject did not appear until 1967.

Comment and discussion after my lectures were invariably fruitful, and I deeply appreciated the patience that my auditors brought to an argument that necessarily reached its conclusion six weeks after it began. Friends outside Berkeley have also contributed substantially to my thinking about fiction. I must give special thanks to Peter Wiseman for sending me, well in advance of publication, the text of the volume entitled *Lies and Fiction in the Ancient World,* which he and Christopher Gill edited together. Without the initiative of Elena Alexeeva I might not have discovered Bulgakov's great novel in time.

I should say that I presented the material on Philoctetes (Chapter III) in a preliminary form at a colloquium organized in 1991 by Siegfried Jäkel on the island of Seili, off the coast of Turku in Finland. The publication of that colloquium, *Power and Spirit* (Annales Universitatis Turkuensis, ser. B, vol. 199, 1993), includes a brief synopsis of my paper on page 63. The substance of Appendix B was offered to the Historia Augusta Colloquium held in Geneva in 1991. The first of my Sather Lectures was delivered, outside the series, as an independent presentation at the University of California in Los Angeles in late 1991.

During my stay in Berkeley a vast and terrifying fire swept over the Oakland hills, disrupting lives and destroying homes. Many Berkeley colleagues lived there. I offered to cancel my third lecture, which was scheduled for the second day after the fire was brought under control; but students and professors alike wanted to proceed with the normal and proper work of the university. That lecture was (and is) largely devoted to the endurance of suffering. I can never forget the strength that I saw in the eyes of those who listened to me that night.

G. W. Bowersock

14 June 1993

Abbreviations

Most abbreviations will be clear from the form of citation, but the following conventional abbreviations should be noted.

AC	*L'Antiquité Classique*
CQ	*Classical Quarterly*
CR	*Classical Review*
CSCO	*Corpus Scriptorum Christianorum Orientalium*
FGH	F. Jacoby, ed., *Die Fragmente der griechischen Historiker*
FHG	C. Müller, ed., *Fragmenta Historicorum Graecorum*
GRBS	*Greek, Roman, and Byzantine Studies*
IGR	*Inscriptiones Graecae ad Res Romanas Pertinentes*
ILS	*Inscriptiones Latinae Selectae*
JAOS	*Journal of the American Oriental Society*
JHS	*Journal of Hellenic Studies*
JRS	*Journal of Roman Studies*

MH	*Museum Helveticum*
NM	*Numismatiska Meddelanden*
OGIS	*Orientis Graeci Inscriptiones Selectae*
PIR²	*Prosopographia Imperii Romani*, 2d ed.
PLRE	*Prosopography of the Later Roman Empire*
RAC	*Reallexikon für Antike und Christentum*
RE	A. von Pauly, G. Wissowa, and W. Kroll, eds., *Realencyclopädie der classischen Altertumswissenschaft*
TAPA	*Transactions of the American Philological Association*

CHAPTER ONE

Truth in Lying

In the second century of our era, probably in the final decade of the reign of the philosophic emperor Marcus Aurelius (the years from 170 to 180), two very different Greek writers addressed a problem that conspicuously unsettled thoughtful people of the time. These writers both struggled to sort out truth from fiction in a world that seemed hopelessly to intermingle and confuse them, a world in which the boundaries between creative imagination and willful mendacity, between fiction and lying, often proved impossible to determine. At least from the age of Homer the history of the Mediterranean lands had been so encrusted with myth and legend that the Greeks and Romans, who came to control that world, found it hard to distinguish corrosion from the hard core. The time of the heroes merged with the achievements of Solon and Cleisthenes, and Romulus, Remus, and Numa were the predecessors of the Gracchi and Cicero. If a sophisticated author was aware of the difference, as Plutarch seemed to be when he undertook his biography of the Athenian hero Theseus, his awareness hardly deterred him.[1] He had already written the lives of Romulus and Numa.

1. Plutarch, *Theseus* 1: "Now that I have traversed the period of time that is accessible to probability and supports a history based on facts [τὸν ἐφικτὸν εἰκότι λόγῳ καὶ βάσιμον ἱστορίᾳ πραγμάτων

The problem that confronted those two Greek writers in the time of Marcus Aurelius was therefore not a new one. But in their day it acquired a special urgency because apparent fictions about both past and present were proliferating at a rate that the classical world had scarcely seen before. The ease of communication and transport in the Roman empire meant that local marvels were local no more. They soon merged into an international conglomerate of fantasy and the supernatural. History was being invented all over again; even the mythic past was being rewritten, and the present was awash in so many miracles and marvels that not even the credulous or the pious could swallow them all.

The two Greek writers gave their works strikingly similar titles. Celsus, an eloquent and venomous pagan apologist, entitled his *A True Discourse* (Ἀληθὴς Λόγος), and Lucian, the most imaginative and stylish satirist that the ancient world ever produced, entitled his, an effervescent fantasy, *True Stories* (Ἀληθῆ Διηγήματα). This latter work is perhaps better known to students of literature by its conventional Latin title, *Vera Historia (True History)*. What is important is that these two contemporary writers chose to signal the issue of truth as they did: "True Λόγος" and "True Διηγήματα." The fiction or lies that exercised them could not have been more different. Yet their

---

ἐχομένη χρόνον], I might well say of earlier periods, 'What lies beyond is full of marvels and unreality, a land of poets and fabulists, of doubt and obscurity.'" After acknowledging that he has already gone back to Lycurgus and Numa, he now asks whom he should pair with Romulus, whose life he has recently written. His choice is Theseus. "May I therefore succeed in purifying the mythic [τὸ μυθῶδες]," he asks, "while making it submit to reason [λόγῳ] and take on the look of history [ἱστορίας ὄψιν]."

targets represented two extremities of the same spectrum of fabrication.

The fiction and mendacity that Celsus wished to expose in his *True Discourse* were nothing less than the Christian representation of the life and death of Jesus Christ. "We must examine this question," wrote Celsus, "whether anyone who really died ever rose again with the same body."[2] Celsus knew of course all the pagan parallels to the resurrection, but he considered them no less fiction than the story of Jesus itself. After all, as Celsus observed, Jesus did not help himself when he was alive, and yet (to quote Celsus's text), "after death he rose again and showed the marks of his punishment and how his hands had been pierced. But who saw this? A hysterical female, as you say, and perhaps some other one of those who were deluded by the same sorcery, who either dreamt in a certain state of mind and through wishful thinking had hallucinations due to some mistaken notion (an experience which has happened to thousands), or, which is more likely, wanted to impress the others by telling this fantastic tale, and so by this cock-and-bull story to provide a chance for other beggars."[3]

These belligerent words, along with much more of Celsus's text, have fortunately survived because the Christian apologist Origen saw fit a century afterward to offer a detailed refutation of them. The Church itself thereby saw to the preservation of a large part of the *True Discourse,* and it is from Origen we learn that Celsus chose a novelistic setting for his invective. He conjured up a Jew talking to other Jews who had been converted to the teachings of Jesus. It cannot escape the reader's notice that

2. Celsus, quoted in Origen, *Contra Celsum* 2.55, given here and elsewhere in the translation by H. Chadwick, *Origen: Contra Celsum* (Cambridge, 1953).

3. *Ibid.*

Celsus has launched his attack on Christianity by creating a fictional setting of his own. In other words, Celsus has created a fiction in order to expose other people's fiction. Of course he is not claiming that his Jewish interlocutor is a real person. His is the kind of fiction that we clearly know to be fiction. But he saw in the Gospel stories another order of fabrication in which there was a claim to historical truth. The truth of Celsus's discourse obviously does not lie in his scenario but in what is said in the scenario. The alleged truth is embedded in the fiction, and Origen understood this perfectly well.

By contrast, the satirist Lucian, although aware of the Christians of his time, was hardly concerned with them when he wrote his *True Stories*. But he was as much concerned as Celsus with the disappearance of traditional boundaries and markers between veracity and falsehood. His *True Stories* are all sheer fantasy, delightful to read and wildly improbable. They include a voyage to the moon, a sojourn in the belly of a whale, and a visit to the illustrious dead. Lucian draws on literary traditions as old as Homer and pays explicit homage to his ancient predecessors in the art of narrating the fabulous, Ctesias of Cnidos and Herodotus, the Father of History.[4] These two classic writers had spawned generations of other fabulous tale tellers and paradoxographers, all of whom served as Lucian's antecedents. Lucian himself said that the knowledgeable reader would be able to detect allusions to his many predecessors in what he was writing.[5] So Lucian's *True Stories* are meant clearly as a literary

---

4. Lucian, *Vera Hist.* 1.3 (Ctesias and Homer), and 2.31 on those who told lies when they were alive, Ctesias and Herodotus being named explicitly.

5. *Ibid.* 1.2: τῶν ἱστορουμένων ἕκαστον οὐκ ἀκωμῳδήτως ᾔνικ-ται πρός τινας τῶν παλαιῶν ποιητῶν τε καὶ συγγραφέων καὶ φιλοσόφων πολλὰ τεράστια καὶ μυθώδη συγγεγραφότων.

entertainment in the first instance. As he wrote in his opening lines, serious literary people ought to relax from time to time with "such works as not only afford wit, charm, and distraction, pure and simple, but also provoke some degree of cultured reflection [οὐκ ἄμουσος θεωρία]."[6]

Now cultured reflection points to a more serious aspect of the fantastic tales that Lucian has cheekily chosen to designate *True Stories*. The one thing they are not is true.[7] Lucian is very candid about this. "I had no true story to relate," he declared, "since nothing worth mentioning had ever happened to me, and consequently I turned to romancing. But I am much more sensible about it than others are, for I will say one thing that *is* true, and that is that I am a liar. . . . My readers must not believe a word I say." Reincarnating the Cretan paradox of Epimenides, Lucian declares that the only true statement in his work is that he is a liar, and he knows perfectly well that this means that the reader has no basis for believing that statement either.

Lucian tries to pull down the distinction between fiction that we accept as fiction and fiction that is presented as a record of

6. *Ibid.*

7. *Ibid.* 1.4. The self-consciously false claim to truth in a clearly fabulous narrative recurs in a great twentieth-century work that owes perhaps even more to Lucian than to Gogol (its more obvious inspiration): M. Bulgakov, *The Master and Margarita*. At the end of Book 1 we read, "The time is approaching to move into the second half of this true story." In the first chapter of Book 2 a sentence begins, "I, the truthful narrator, yet a mere onlooker. . . ." (Note that Lucian's *Vera Historia* is also in two books.) The extreme, often grotesque fantasies of Bulgakov create a vivid feeling of life in Moscow in the 1920s and 1930s, and the suppression of this novel by Soviet authorities for more than twenty years after the author's death in 1940 is proof of its historical truth despite its literal absurdities. Much the same could probably be said of Lucian's *Vera Historia* as a document of its time.

real events. Everything, by his own admission, is lies. Yet what Lucian describes inevitably reflects, all too obviously, the world in which he lives. This can be no accident. The people of the moon are at war with the people of the sun, but eventually they conclude a peace treaty that mirrors in its terms and language, as well as in the oath that concludes it, the traditional peace treaties of the Greeks. The games of the dead in the underworld are a faithful reflection of the athletic and literary competitions that were the pride of the great Greek cities of the Roman empire.[8] Aristophanes and Homer are given reverential treatment that reflects their position in Lucian's own day.[9] All this means that when Lucian claims that his *True Stories* are all lies, that paradoxical claim itself must be included among the lies. Nor should this be surprising, inasmuch as falsehoods are always an integral part of the world in which they are disseminated. This is a truth that is as important for historians as for politicians.

It is symptomatic of the time that both Celsus and Lucian should proclaim truth even as they immerse themselves in fiction, that they should attack fiction by creating fiction, that they should confuse lies and admitted fabrication. Lucian makes it clear that it would surely be reassuring to his cultivated readers to know at the outset that what they are reading is all mendacious. Yet, as they read on, they discover that in some respects

8. On all this, see the magisterial study by Louis Robert, "Lucien en son temps," in *À travers l'Asie Mineure* (1980), pp. 393–436, esp. 427–32 on *Vera Historia* ("Le concours dans l'Île des Bienheureux"). See also C. P. Jones, *Culture and Society in Lucian* (1986), pp. 52–55.

9. Aristophanes: Lucian, *Vera Hist.* 1.29: "a wise and truthful man, whose works arouse undeserved disbelief" (in Reardon's excellent translation). For Homer, see esp. *Vera Hist.* 2.15 ("Homer's poetry being very popular"), and 2.20 on Homer's birthplace as "a bone of contention on earth to this very day."

it is not. This is the reverse of the experience of readers like Celsus confronted with the Gospel narratives. There they are under the impression that this is an accurate record of what happened, but, as they read on, they have the disquieting feeling that some of it may or must be mendacious. Celsus and Lucian thus give us two sides of the same coin, and this coin is perhaps the most important currency in the intellectual commerce of the Roman Empire.

Homer, Herodotus, Ctesias, Xenophon (in his account of the education of Cyrus), and many other engaging and less than reliable narrators had been familiar for centuries in classical antiquity. Myths and legends existed in a bewildering variety of forms. Hellenistic scholars at Alexandria were well employed in trying to sort them out. But, despite the protestations of Hecataeus long ago, who advanced his own claims to truth by denouncing the absurdity of what the Greeks were saying, fiction did not seem to be a problem.[10] In the first century B.C., Cicero could proclaim Herodotus with equanimity as the Father of History and then go on to denounce him as the author of innumerable fabulous tales.[11] History had simply become the plot—what happened or what was said to have happened. It was different from biography, as Plutarch and others struggled to demonstrate;[12] it was the received account of the past that reached back into mythical times without a break. For Herod-

10. Hecateus of Miletus, *FGH* I.A.1, F 1(a): Ἑκαταῖος Μιλήσιος ὧδε μυθεῖται· τάδε γράφω, ὥς μοι δοκεῖ ἀληθέα εἶναι· οἱ γὰρ Ἑλλήνων λόγοι πολλοί τε καὶ γελοῖοι, ὡς ἐμοὶ φαίνονται, εἰσίν.

11. Cicero, *De Legibus* 1.5: "et apud Herodotum, patrem historiae, et apud Theopompum sunt innumerabiles fabulae."

12. Cf. the celebrated opening of Plutarch's *Alexander* (1.2): οὔτε γὰρ ἱστορίας γράφομεν, ἀλλὰ βίους. See also C. B. R. Pelling, "Truth and Fiction in Plutarch's *Lives*," in *Antonine Literature*, ed. D. A. Russell (1990), pp. 19–52.

otus the word ἱστορία could mean a serious investigation or piece of research, but for the later Greeks and all the residents of the Roman empire, the word generally meant the story as it was known and told—the plot. Disruptions of history in this sense could therefore be highly disturbing, breaking the familiar patterns that linked past with present, and, at the same time, signaling changes for the future. The violation of history as plot or the rewriting of it constituted a rupture in the cultural tradition.

In a small but telling way an epigram of the Greek satiric poet Lucillius, from the time of the emperor Nero, illustrates this whole process. The poet addresses a dancer of female roles who afforded general pleasure to viewers by performing mythological ballets according to the stories that everyone knew: πάντα καθ' ἱστορίην ὀρχούμενος, "you danced everything according to the story."[13] But the satirist is vexed—very vexed—by the dancer's failure to enact the suicide of a figure who was well known to have killed herself after an incestuous affair with her brother. "You had a sword," says the poet, "but yet left the stage alive: that was not according to the story" (τοῦτο παρ' ἱστορίην).

This poem had a conspicuous resonance in the work of Martial, a Latin satiric poet of the next generation. Among the epigrams he wrote to commemorate the opening of the great Roman amphitheater that we know today as the Colosseum are some lines describing a representation of Orpheus on the stage.[14] Everyone knew, and presumably still knows, that Orpheus charmed the animals with his beautiful music. The Roman production staff created fabulous stage machinery, so, as Martial put it, "cliffs crept by and marvelous woods sped swiftly on." We read that every kind of wild beast was there, and Orpheus himself

13. *Anth. Pal.* 11.254.
14. Martial, *Lib. Spectac.* 1.21.

made his music as birds hovered overhead. But then a bear came out and tore him to pieces. This surprising dénouement, a poor recognition of Orpheus's musical talent, constitutes the point of Martial's epigram: *haec tantum res est facta* παρ' ἱστορίαν, "this thing alone was done not according to the story."[15]

Rewriting the past—the intrusion of fiction into what was taken to be history—becomes from this period of Lucillius and Martial an increasingly conspicuous feature of the Graeco-Roman world. Origen strained every nerve in the third century to confute Celsus's elaborate attempt to expose the Gospel narratives as fiction, and yet he had to admit that fabrication had already thrown the objectivity of what he considered the historical past into considerable doubt. "We are embarrassed," he wrote, "by the fictitious stories which for some unknown reasons are bound up with the opinion, which everyone believes, that there really was a war in Troy between the Greeks and the Trojans."[16] This remark from a man of Origen's consummate learning gives pause. "Everyone believes," he says confidently, "that the Trojan War really took place," but the tradition has been seriously contaminated in his view by the appearance of fictitious stories. In saying this he reflects a general indifference to the distinction between history and myth. And at the same time he reports on a phenomenon that can be well documented— the rewriting of the old stories.[17]

15. For the brilliant and definitive establishment of the text of Martial in this line, see A. E. Housman, "Two Epigrams of Martial," *CR* 15 (1901), 154–55, reprinted in *The Classical Papers of A. E. Housman*, ed. J. Diggle and F. R. D. Goodyear, vol. 2 (1972), pp. 536–38.

16. Origen, *Contra Celsum* 1.42 (trans. H. Chadwick).

17. Note, in this regard, the important observation by J. R. Morgan, "Make-Believe and Make Believe," in *Lies and Fiction in the Ancient*

The dilemma that confronted Origen had troubled the philosophical writer Sextus Empiricus a few generations earlier. Sextus's analysis of the nature of historical or quasi-historical narrative drew on Hellenistic theories best known to us through Cicero, but Sextus formulated the problem in what is perhaps the single most important meditation on fiction and falsity from the time of the Roman empire.[18] In a polemic against the teaching of literature by grammarians in the imperial system of education, Sextus dwells at one point on what he calls "the historical part" (τὸ ἱστορικὸν μέρος) of γραμματική (grammar in the broad, ancient sense). This part of the subject is concerned with narratives, stories that are told—τὰ ἱστορούμενα. According to Sextus there are three kinds of such narratives: history, fiction (πλάσμα), and myth. History, he says, is the presentation (ἔκθεσις) of truths and of what actually happened; πλάσμα, of things that did not happen but resemble things that have happened; myth, of things that did not happen and are false (ψευδῆ), such as stories of the Titans, the Gorgon, or Hecabe turning into a dog.[19] Several times Sextus links together the nonexistent

---

World, ed. C. Gill and T. P. Wiseman (1993), p. 176: "Whereas all novels are fiction, not all fictions are novels."

18. Sextus Emp., *Adversus Math.* 1.263–69. Cf. Cicero, *De Inv.* 1.19.27, as well as Auct. *Ad Herennium* 1.8.13 and Quint. *Inst. Orat.* 2.4.2. My friend Charles Murgia kindly drew my attention also to Servius, *In Aen.* 1.235, and Isid. *Orig.* 1.43.1 for the transmission of the Latin terminology. Cf. the discussion of μῦθος and μίμησις in Arist. *Poetics* 1450ᵃ3–1451ᵇ32.

19. The Latin equivalents for these three kinds of narrative were, at least from Cicero onward (see the previous note), *historia, argumentum,* and *fabula.* For a recent account of πλάσμα/πλάττειν, see G. Rispoli, *Lo spazio del verisimile: Il raconto, la storia, e il mito* (1988), pp. 142–69.

(ἀγένητα or ἀνύπαρκτα) and the false, even as he raises the issue of truth in plausible fictions.

Sextus directs his polemic against the grammarians for the particular reason that these teachers have not supplied any criteria for determining truth in narrative. That means that it is impossible to say what reports can constitute history, inasmuch as history on his definition must narrate what is true and what has really happened. Furthermore, the absence of criteria for truth also means, as Sextus illustrates in detail, that it is equally impossible to say which divergent myths or fictions (πλάσματα) are true, and which are false. The significance of this criticism is manifest in an age, such as the late second century, so accustomed to the revision of old myths and the fabrication of historical romances. Sextus's criticism also provides the conceptual background that allowed a Lucian to talk about true stories while publicly acknowledging that he was telling lies. Lucian was playing upon the idea that fiction can be—although it is not necessarily—true. This idea was nicely phrased in the last decade by the French scholar Paul Veyne when he wrote, "Men do not find the truth; they create it, as they create their history."[20]

Serious Homeric revisionism spans most of the period of the Roman empire, beginning with several elaborate attempts to invent a pre-Homeric non-Greek perspective on the Trojan War. The works that have survived under the names of Dares the Phrygian and Dictys the Cretan are both important parts of this revisionist effort. Not long before Origen was writing, the sophist Philostratus and the poet Serenus Sammonicus had also taken further steps in this same heretical direction. In the early second century Philo of Byblos had produced a history of the ancient

20. P. Veyne, *Did the Greeks Believe in Their Myths?* trans. P. Wissing (1988), p. xii.

Phoenicians that claimed to be a rendering in Greek of a Semitic account composed before the Trojan War.[21] As Philo liked to point out, his amazing discovery of this venerable text impugned the veracity of all the traditional Greek stories about the Phoenicians. So for a person imbued in classical Greek culture, as the Christian Origen most certainly was, these developments were nothing less than shocking. They also posed problems in trying to prove why the relatively recent, allegedly historical narratives from Palestine should not be construed as fiction when so much else could be.

For any coherent and persuasive interpretation of the Roman empire it becomes obvious that fiction must be viewed as a part of its history. We have long grown accustomed to hearing of late that history itself is a fiction, or rhetoric, or whatever. The ancients would not have found that a particularly surprising doctrine, inasmuch as they drew only a faint line between myth and history and, as Cicero put it, considered the writing of history an *opus oratorium*—a rhetorical work.[22] But the overt creation of fiction as a means of rewriting or even inventing the

21. See L. Troiani, *L'opera storiografica di Filone da Byblos* (1974). The fragments of Philo may be examined in *FGH* III.C.790. Dares and Dictys will be treated later in this chapter, and Philostratus's *Heroicus* will be taken up in Chapter III. For the *Res Reconditae* of Serenus Sammonicus, cf. Macrob. *Sat.* 3.9.6, with other references cited in G. W. Bowersock, *Greek Sophists in the Roman Empire* (1969), p. 107.

22. Cicero, *De Legibus* 1.5: "quippe cum sit opus, ut tibi quidem videri solet, unum hoc oratorium maxime." In the current debate, Hayden White's *Metahistory* (1973) is still central. Cf. the response by A. Momigliano, "The Rhetoric of History and the History of Rhetoric: On Hayden White's Tropes," *Comparative Criticism: A Year Book,* vol. 3, ed. E. S. Shaffer (1981), pp. 259–68, reprinted in *Settimo contributo alla storia degli studi classici e del mondo antico* (1984), pp. 49–59.

past was a serious business for many of the ancients, and for us the enormous increase in fictional production of all kinds during the Roman empire poses major questions of historical interpretation. There was as much truth or falsehood in fiction as in history itself. Fiction must necessarily include not only overt works of the imagination, such as the novels and Lucian's *True Stories*, but also the rewriting of the mythic and legendary past as part of the creation of a new and miraculous present. As Sextus Empiricus shows, all this belonged to the class of narratives (τὰ ἱστορούμενα), comprising realistic fiction and myths no less than history.

The immense body of fictional narratives that we tend to call novels today must be seen within this larger context of fabrication and rewriting. Some of these narratives are set in remote historical times, others in the present, but all are eloquent and detailed witnesses to the age in which they were composed. If they do not purport to be a historical record of facts in the same way as the Trojan narrative of Dictys the Cretan or the Christian Gospels, they nonetheless constitute a rich and essential part of any history that we might wish to write of the time in which they were composed. Nor are the novels themselves homogeneous. The Greek romances offer a look into the diverse and far-flung societies of the Mediterranean world that is very different from the much more narrow perspectives of the Latin writers Petronius and Apuleius (despite the probable Greek antecedents of both).

The richness and importance of fiction for the historian of the Roman empire has been little investigated or appreciated. This neglect seems largely to have been the result of the way philologists and literary critics handled it. For one thing the novels have tended to be studied independently of other fictional forms. In 1876 Erwin Rohde published his pioneering work *Der griechische Roman*, opening up the whole field and exploring it with

Fiction as History

exceptional learning and clarity. But instead of provoking further work as creative as his own, Rohde's book only brought
forth generations of scholarly sheep that either followed along
faithfully or turned the other way but nonetheless lived entirely
in dependence upon their shepherd. There were two principal
problems in Rohde's conceptual scheme: first, he isolated the
genre of the novel from everything else, and second, he over-
emphasized the problem of origins or antecedents of extant
works. With works of imaginative literature there is nothing
more ruinous for historical understanding than genre theory or
a mindless search for antecedents, origins, and distant parallels.
If Rohde could connect the Greek novel with tales of travel and
Hellenistic eroticism (as he did) and throw in a generous dosage
of rhetoric of the so-called Second Sophistic (as he did), he
thought that in that way he had actually explained and interpreted the phenomenon of the Greek novel. Papyri subsequently
proved the barrenness of his method by revealing that he had
presupposed dates for the extant works that were far too late—
erroneous by several centuries.[23]

Yet Rohde's schematic handling of the novels was infinitely
better than the interpretations of his critics, of whom Eduard
Schwartz is a good representative.[24] Schwartz, like Wilamowitz
(who applauded Schwartz's lectures on the Greek novel), had so
firm a preconception as to what Hellenism was that he was
incapable of understanding it.[25] He believed that all novelistic

23. Cf. E. Bowie, "The Greek Novel," in *Cambridge History of
Classical Literature*, vol. 1 (1985), pp. 683–99.

24. E. Schwartz, *Fünf Vorträge über den griechischen Roman*, with
an introduction by A. Rehm, 2d ed. (1943).

25. U. von Wilamowitz in *Deutsche Literaturzeitung* 23 (1902),
3219, claiming that Schwartz had destroyed the foundations of Rohde's
work. Cf. M. H. Chambers, *Georg Busolt: His Career in Letters*,

fiction was completely un-Greek and had to be explained by degenerate influences either from the Latin West, as in the case of Petronius, or from the Semitic East, as in the case of Lucian and others. For Schwartz, who declared that true Hellenism among the Syrians penetrated no farther than their epidermis or that Greeks in Italy found an alien growth in their garden, the Graeco-Roman world and the Greeks themselves could only be grotesquely misrepresented.[26]

Prose fiction needs to be considered in a broad context, broader than the novel alone. To talk, as some do, of the world of the *Golden Ass* or the world of the Greek novel is to suggest that these works somehow have a separate, self-contained world of their own, whereas they ought to be seen as *part* of something larger, which is the Graeco-Roman empire. It is certainly necessary, as a first step, to identify the explicit historical references that can be captured and identified in works of fiction. Fergus Millar has done this expertly for Apuleius.[27] But this can be only a beginning. All these fictional works deserve to be considered in relation to a larger, kaleidoscopic historical context.

In the last few decades the novels have attracted the attention of a vigorous battalion of literary scholars, but not even their work has much percolated to literary criticism outside the clas-

---

Mnemosyne Supplement 113 (1990), p. 59, n. 49. Of course, Wilamowitz had a deeply rooted antipathy to Rohde because of the quarrel over Nietzsche and Wagner.

26. Cf. Schwartz (n. 24 above), pp. 149–50: "die gewandten, ehrgeizigen Syrer, denen das Echthellenische nur bis zur Epidermis ging. . . ." It is hardly surprising that Schwartz's lectures were reprinted appreciatively in 1943.

27. F. Millar, "The World of the *Golden Ass*," *JRS* 71 (1981), 63–75.

sical field. As Bryan Reardon observed recently, Northrop Frye, in his important book on romance as a kind of secular scripture, seemed blissfully unaware of one of the most important and probably the earliest of the extant ancient novelists.[28] If Lucian and Sextus Empiricus serve to illustrate the complexity and significance of the growth of fiction in the second century, the emperor Julian, in the fourth, shows himself no less preoccupied with the problem. He complains in his puritanical way about a renewed popularity of fictional works composed in earlier times in the form of history: ἐν ἱστορίας εἴδει . . . πλάσματα.[29] That word πλάσματα was, as we have seen in Sextus, the standard expression for fictions in Greek of this period, and it was also closely associated with dramatic works for the theater as well as with prose narratives.

Drama as we know it was, of course, another traditional area of literary fabrication, but the conventions of the stage and the verse in which the plays were written made them less easily assimilated to narrative history. Yet the scenes, dénouements, and emotional excitements of the two genres could be remarkably similar. Heliodorus's Ethiopian romance is shot through, as many have recognized, with the language and conventions of the stage.[30] In Greek the verbs for "to make comedy" and "to make tragedy" (κωμῳδεῖν and τραγῳδεῖν) could be used without strain simply to mean "making fun of" something and "making grandiose exaggerations." In a memorable passage in the writings of Galen from the mid-second century, the great doctor

---

28. B. P. Reardon, *The Form of Greek Romance* (1991), p. 17, with reference to N. Frye, *The Secular Scripture: A Study of the Structure of Romance* (1976). Frye totally disregarded Chariton.

29. Julian, *Epist.* 89b, 301b (Bidez).

30. E.g., S. Bartsch, *Decoding the Ancient Novel* (1989), p. 129.

discusses the cleverness of nature in making the body work as it does—to such a degree that, if you hadn't actually seen a particular healing take place, you would think that someone was making it all up rather than telling the truth.[31] The verbs that he uses are τραγῳδεῖν, "to make tragedy," and ἀληθεύειν, "to tell the truth," clearly to express the idea of making something up in a grandiose way rather than telling the truth. This is once again the opposition between fiction and truth, expressed here by a striking theatrical term. Similarly Lucian finds no problem in using the verb κωμῳδεῖν, "to make comedies," as an expression for satirizing people.[32]

The second-century author of a remarkable book on the interpretation of dreams, Artemidorus of Daldis, illustrates even better this point about the relation between fictions (πλάσματα) and drama.[33] He considers the interesting situation in which the dreamer imagines that he is composing (or perhaps performing in) a tragedy, or that he holds in his hands the text of some tragedies or some πλάσματα (τραγικὰ ἔχειν δράματα ἢ πλάσματα). The passage has given interpreters considerable trouble, and variant readings have been proposed; but πλάσματα is clearly what Artemidorus wrote, as the new Arabic translation of a lost Greek manuscript of his work proves once and for all.[34] These πλάσματα or "fictions" cannot be the same as the plays, because those are described as δράματα—τραγικὰ

31. Galen, *De Usu Partium* 16.4, 286 (p. 392, 1. 16 Helmreich).
32. Lucian, *Pisc.* 25.
33. Artemidorus, *Oneir.* 1.56, p. 63 (Pack).
34. T. Fahd, ed., *Artémidore d'Ephèse: Le livre des songes*, Institut Français de Damas (1964), p. 117 (Arabic), *sanāᶜa*. Fahd's own Arabic translation of the Greek text shows that he has missed the problem here. See Appendix A below.

δράματα. What we have here, without any doubt, is a reference to fictional novels of a tragic character. Artemidorus goes on to describe the features of the works that the dreamer is dreaming about. They include, among other horrendous experiences, enslavements, battles, and rapes, all of which, as readers of Greek novels will know, are absolutely standard fare for these works. The close connection between what we call drama and fiction is manifestly the reason why the very word δρᾶμα comes to mean "prose fiction" in early and middle Byzantine Greek. The development of the sense is perfectly natural. In the ninth century the patriarch Photius can describe the character of a work of Greek fiction without ambiguity simply by the words δραμα- τικὸν οἱ λόγοι, "the stories are a novel [or romance]."[35]

Artemidorus is an equally good witness for the relation of prose fiction to comic theater. After dispatching dreamers who dream of tragedy or tragic works, he contemplates those who dream of composing (or acting in) comedies. In this case he is careful to separate Old Comedy from New.[36] In other words he distinguishes the obscene and explicitly insulting style of comedy we associate with Aristophanes from the more gentle domestic comedies with their stereotyped characters that we associate with Menander. Once again, this time with both styles of comedy, he

---

35. Photius, *Biblioth.* 109a [166], p. 140, l. 7 (Henry), on Antonius Diogenes. The discussion of δρᾶμα and δραματικόν in E. Rohde, *Der griechische Roman und seine Vorläufer*, 3d ed. (1914), p. 376, n. 1, is still valuable. For a recent study, not uniformly persuasive but very useful, see N. Marini, "Δρᾶμα. Possible denominazione per il romanzo greco d'amore," *Studi Italiani di Filologia Classica*, ser. 3, 9 (1991), 232–43.

36. Artemidorus, *loc. cit.* (n. 33 above): τὰ μὲν τῆς παλαιᾶς κωμῳδίας σκώμματα . . . , τὰ δὲ τῆς καθ' ἡμᾶς κωμῳδίας.

mentions the existence of πλάσματα, that is to say, "comic fictions."[37] As in the case of tragedy, these fictions are clearly not plays. No one would deny that comic fiction in the Roman empire—as best represented by Petronius's hilarious and obscene novel *The Satyricon,* and the fantasies of Lucian in his *True Stories*—is deeply indebted to the satiric writings that preceded it; and satire had its own roots deep in comedy, as the Latin poet Horace explicitly declared in one of his most memorable satiric poems. There he singled out Eupolis, Cratinus, and Aristophanes, the three great masters of the Old Comedy—the comedy of obscenity and explicit mockery of individuals.[38] In fact, Artemidorus's recognition of the tradition of comic fictions in a context that also invokes Old Comedy calls attention to a change in literary taste in the second half of the first century and the beginning of the second. That is a return to enthusiasm for the Aristophanic style after several centuries in which Menandrian New Comedy was all the fashion. In the early second century the younger Pliny alludes to a friend, a playwright called Vergilius Romanus, who is said to have abandoned his former habit of writing plays in the style of Menander to devote himself henceforth to Old Comedy—that is, original work in the style of Old Comedy.[39]

37. For the reading, the Arabic version is again our witness (cf. n. 34 above). See Appendix A.

38. Hor. *Serm.* 1.4.1: *Eupolis atque Cratinus Aristophanesque poetae.*

39. Pliny, *Epist.* 6.21.2–5, esp. 2, "Nuper audivi Vergilium Romanum paucis legentem comoediam ad exemplar veteris comoediae scriptam," and 5, "Nunc primum se in vetere comoedia, sed non tamquam inciperet ostendit." A. N. Sherwin-White's commentary *ad loc.* in *The Letters of Pliny* (1966), p. 381, is confused. Cf. Marcus Aurelius, *Ad Se Ipsum* 11.6 in praise of Old Comedy.

Literary scholars have tended to miss altogether this interesting phenomenon of the original composition of Old Comedy during the time of the Roman empire. The novelist Antonius Diogenes, who must have been an approximate contemporary of Vergilius Romanus, is also known to have written Old Comedy, by his own assertion as preserved in the writings of Photius. Unfortunately his explicit remark has been missed or misinterpreted by those who failed to recognize the nature of Greek dramatic writing at this late date.[40] Diogenes, in fact, embodies the nexus between drama and fiction. In the romance of Leucippe and Cleitophon by Achilles Tatius, a work that had certainly been written by the end of the second century, one of the more admirable speakers in the courtroom episode at the end of that novel makes a stunning impact because, we are told, he imitates the comedy of Aristophanes (τὴν Ἀριστοφάνους ἐζηλωκὼς κωμῳδίαν).[41] This means that he spoke his courtroom rhetoric using the mannerisms and satire associated with Aristophanic comedy. And, sure enough, Achilles Tatius goes on to describe the speech of this orator as delivered with urbanity and sarcastic wit.

Among the true stories that Lucian tells for the delectation of his readers is a visit to no less a place than the Cloudcuckooland (Νεφελοκοκκυγία) invented by Aristophanes in *The Birds*.[42] This tribute to the great playwright of the fifth century B.C. is underscored when Lucian remarks that his sight of the mirac-

---

40. Photius, *Biblioth.* 111a [166], p. 147, ll. 34–35 (Henry): Λέγει δὲ ἑαυτὸν ὅτι ποιητής ἐστι κωμῳδίας παλαιᾶς. Henry translates absurdly, "Il se dit le narrateur d'une intrigue ancienne." In the new English rendering by G. N. Sandy, in B. P. Reardon, ed., *Collected Ancient Greek Novels* (1989), we find (p. 781): "He says of himself that he is the author of an ancient story."

41. Achill. Tat. *Leuc. and Clit.* 8.9.

42. Lucian, *Vera Hist.* 1.29.

ulous place reminded him of Aristophanes the poet, whom he calls "a wise and truthful man, whose works have aroused undeserved disbelief."[43] To call Aristophanes wise and truthful, particularly with reference to Cloudcuckooland, is obviously insouciant but entirely consistent with the tenor of the *True Stories*. The remark turns upon the ancient view that fictions could be true. The praise of Aristophanes here is, despite Lucian's denigration of the opponents of Old Comedy, an entirely plausible index of the tastes and controversies of his time and, in particular, of the important relationship between Aristophanes' theater and the practitioners of fiction. We have here another example of the truth in Lucian's self-proclaimed lying.

If we step back to take a broader view of the fictional production of the Roman empire, it becomes apparent that this vast output encompassed four major types: fantastic tales, Homeric revisionism, tragic or romantic novels, and comic or satiric novels. These types were not necessarily exclusive. Homeric revisionism could easily accommodate tragedy or romance, and so could the fantastic or miraculous tales. Some fictions proclaimed their character openly, and some did not. It was, as Celsus and Origen discovered, often very difficult to separate fact from fiction, especially when an author had, either seriously or playfully, adopted a pose of historical veracity. All this had, as is often observed, many and varied antecedents in the classical literature and traditions of earlier centuries—in epic, in drama, in mythography, in travelers' tales, and perhaps even in a few romantic narratives about famous legendary characters such as Ninus and Semiramis or the biblical Joseph and Asenath.[44]

43. *Ibid.*

44. For the so-called Ninus Romance, see Sandy (n. 40 above), pp. 803–8, with bibliography. On Joseph and Asenath, see Stephanie West,

But there can be no denying that the explosion of fiction in the Roman empire represents something quite new. It is a part of the history of that time, in all probability not an insignificant part. Although it is hard to discover why it arose and what were the sources of its popularity and diffusion, it is not so difficult to see when it all began. That may ultimately provide a clue as to why it began. The beginning of the massive proliferation of fiction can be assigned pretty clearly to the reign of the emperor Nero, in the middle of the first century of the Christian era.

Nero was eccentric in many ways, but among his least destructive passions was his enthusiasm for literature and the arts. (He wrote poetry himself and performed on stage.) He encouraged the Greeks with a passion. Even the gentle Plutarch, who knew the worst about Nero, had to admit at one point that he deserved some favorable consideration because he was a philhellene.[45] It is perhaps not surprising, therefore, that his reign witnessed a resurgence of Greek creativity in literature as well as the metamorphosis of Greek comic themes in the Latin novel of Petronius. The reign of Nero has left four distinct markers for the evolution of fiction in the centuries that lay ahead. The first of these is Lucillius, the Greek satiric poet who influenced Martial later. The second is his contemporary Petronius, with whom he shared an exceptional mastery of the fantastic and the absurd. This will become apparent as we proceed, but it suffices now to say that the conjunction of Lucillius and Petronius under Nero laid the foundation for the comic πλάσματα to which Artemidorus referred a century later.

"*Joseph and Asenath:* A Neglected Greek Romance," *CQ* 24 (1974), 70–81.

45. Plut. *De Sera Num. Vind.* 32, 567F–568A: τῶν ὑπηκόων τὸ βέλτιστον καὶ θεοφιλέστατον γένος ἠλευθέρωσε.

The third marker is the pre-Homeric Trojan fiction ascribed to Dictys of Crete, who allegedly fought in the Trojan War. It is entirely a fabrication of the Neronian period. The work, in Phoenician allegedly, was supposed to have been discovered in a box and made known to Nero when he was visiting Greece.[46] It was promptly translated from the original Phoenician into Greek, and today we possess not only a complete Latin translation of the Greek but even a papyrus fragment with some of the Greek text itself.[47] It goes without saying that the Greek was actually the original text created for the delectation of Nero, the Homerist, Hellenist, and patron of letters. The narration of Dictys turned Homer on his head, just as did another piece of fiction undoubtedly concocted later under the name of Dares the Phrygian.[48] Rewriting the Homeric stories was to become a fad. The amazing discovery of a pre-Homeric text in Phoenician, which was promptly disseminated in Greek, was to recur once again, only a generation or so after Dictys, in the history of Philo of Byblos.[49]

Of the four Neronian markers, Lucillius, Petronius, and Dictys are at least tolerably well known to students of the period. The fourth has almost been forgotten. That is a great pity. He was a forward-looking personality, although he perhaps did not realize

46. Dictys Cret. *Ephem.*, *epist.* and *prolog.* See now S. Merkle, "Telling the True Story of the Trojan War: The Eyewitness Account of Dictys of Crete," in *The Search for the Ancient Novel*, ed. J. Tatum (1994), pp. 183–96.

47. The opening of the Latin version shows that this translation is of Severan date. For fragments of the Greek, *P. Tebt.* 268; *P. Oxy.* 2539.

48. We possess the work ascribed to Dares (*De Excidio Troiae*) in a Latin version from late antiquity, with a fictitious dedication to Cornelius Nepos by Sallust.

49. See n. 21 above.

it. He is Ptolemaeus Chennus—Ptolemy called, for reasons we shall never be able to discover, "the Quail." He was a man who shared the lunatic imagination of a Lucillius or a Petronius and combined it with the rich fantasy of the author of the work ascribed to Dictys of Crete. He told lies as easily as he breathed, he adored the paradoxical and the miraculous, and he saw Homer as an arch-rival. In the whole history of imperial fiction there is no personality who combines so fully the talents of deadpan mendacity, Homeric revisionism, and extravagant narration. The Quail is truly an embodiment of fiction, and yet—for good or ill—he inhabited and undeniably reflected the real world.

Ptolemy the Quail, son of Hephaestion, came from Alexandrian Egypt and made his career in Rome as a grammarian. He must have been the youngest of the four Neronian figures, since he taught and wrote at Rome from the time of Nero until the early second century. He was numbered among the great educators of the age.[50] Among his works, all of which are now lost, three are known to us by title in the entry on him in the *Suda*, and there is an extensive summary of one of them in the writings of the patriarch Photius.[51] Each of the three works represents a significant departure in Greek and Roman literary taste. The work read by Photius was an extensive prose account of ancient mythology. It was entitled most appropriately *The Paradoxical History* (Παράδοξος Ἱστορία). It was also known as the *New*

---

50. *Suda* s.v. Ἐπαφρόδιτος Χαιρωνεύς, who flourished at Rome from Nero to Nerva, καθ᾽ ὃν χρόνον καὶ Πτολεμαῖος ὁ Ἡφαιστίωνος ἦν καὶ ἄλλοι συχνοὶ τῶν ὀνομαστῶν ἐν παιδείᾳ. Cf. *Suda* s.v. Πτολεμαῖος Ἀλεξανδρεύς, γραμματικός, ὁ τοῦ Ἡφαιστίωνος, γεγονὼς ἐπί τε Τραιανοῦ καὶ Ἀδριανοῦ τῶν αὐτοκρατόρων, προσαγορευθεὶς δὲ Χέννος.

51. Photius, *Biblioth.* 146a (*ad fin.*) – 153b [190], pp. 51–72 (Henry).

History (Καινὴ Ἱστορία). Both titles reflect the fact that it contained (as Photius demonstrates in many pages of summary) a completely irresponsible rewriting of many of the famous stories of the past. All this was accomplished with a completely straight face and in a pose of scholarly precision. Countless authorities were cited for the rectifications advanced, but it has long been apparent that almost all these alleged authorities are known only through Ptolemy the Quail and are mentioned by no one else. It is perfectly clear that he simply made them up. A number of the stories have strong romantic elements and make good reading on their own account. The whole must have been a dazzling *tour de force*. The popularity of Ptolemy's work may well be reflected in another of the compositions of Philo of Byblos, who seems to have been remarkably attuned to the latest literary trends. He too wrote a *Paradoxical History*.[52] Ptolemy's writing in this genre obviously gave a ninth-century patriarch like Photius a severe case of indigestion.

His other two important works are known to us only by title and a short description preserved in the *Suda* lexicon. But this meager information is of the greatest interest. Ptolemy wrote a poem in twenty-four books with the polemical title of Ἀνθόμηρος, in other words, *The Anti-Homer Poem*—a confrontation of Homer on his own poetic turf. The other lost work bore an enigmatic title, simply *Sphinx;* but perhaps it is not so enigmatic for an author coming from Alexandria. The piece is described by the *Suda* as, in Greek, δρᾶμα ἱστορικόν, which Albrecht Dihle has persuasively interpreted to mean a romance or romantic novel.[53] Certainly the word δρᾶμα in the Greek of the *Suda,* combined with the word for telling stories (ἱστορικόν),

52. *FGH* III.C.790, F 12–13.
53. A. Dihle, *RE* 23.2, col. 1862.

should mean that we are to interpret this as a narrative of some sort. It would be difficult to say on so little evidence what kind of narrative this was, but it might well have been a romance about the great legendary figures of Ptolemy's homeland, Egypt. We possess already on papyrus a substantial fragment of an Egyptian romance associated with the goddess Tefnut, in which Egyptian fiction is presented in the modes of Greek storytelling known to us in the extant novels.⁵⁴ Ptolemy the Quail has a good claim to being among the leaders in this kind of literature.

We know from Photius that Ptolemy dedicated his *Paradoxical History* to a certain Julia Tertulla.⁵⁵ This exiguous information is quite enough to confirm his high standing in Roman society of the period. Tertullus (or Tertulla for a woman) is a name that surfaces conspicuously in Roman onomastics toward the end of the first century and the first decades of the second, which is exactly the time of Ptolemy's later years on earth. This Julia Tertulla ought perhaps to be identified with a high degree of probability from an inscription in Asia Minor, where a woman of this name is revealed as the sister of the wife of a consul of the year 100.⁵⁶ One might have expected the aging Quail also to have known the equally aging satirist Martial, who survived into the era of felicity after the tyranny of Domitian. It is even possible that Martial made fun of his contemporary, master of so many different forms and styles. For at about this time Martial wrote a pungent epigram complaining of verses that were being illicitly circulated under his name, although he judged them far below the

54. *P. Lond.* 274. For discussion of the Tefnut Romance, see R. M. Rattenbury in *New Chapters in the History of Greek Literature, Third Series*, ed. J. U. Powell (1933), pp. 226–30.

55. Photius, *Biblioth.* 146b [190], p. 51, l. 10 (Henry).

56. *IGR* 3.562 (Tlos). Cf. *PIR*², I 706, wife of L. Julius Marinus Caecilius Simplex.

quality that any discerning person should have expected in his authentic work. One would not, observed Martial, expect a parrot to speak with the voice of a quail: *voce ut loquatur psittacus coturnicis.*[57] The skill of the parrot was much admired in antiquity: it could imitate the human voice and language. The inhuman sound of a quail left, by contrast, something to be desired.

Ptolemy may not have been a very distinguished writer, but he was undeniably an inventive one. Perhaps the world is no worse off without his writings, but he was a portent. Even as he wrote his fabulous and incredible stories, no less fabulous and incredible stories were beginning to circulate in Palestine and the Greek East. These were the stories of miraculous healings and resurrection that were to exercise Celsus and so many others in the century to come. How was Ptolemy the Quail to tell that these were not the work of a writer like himself?

57. Martial 10.3.7.

CHAPTER TWO

Other Peoples, Other Places

The peace of the Roman empire that Augustus established was purchased by monarchy, but it was a real and enduring peace. It embraced the entire Mediterranean world as no constitutional dispensation had ever done before. It was broken from time to time by imperialist campaigns of annexation, by hostile incursions on the frontier, and by occasional rebellions (of which two in Judaea were by far the most fierce and disruptive). But the unity of the Graeco-Roman world for some two centuries was essentially unquestioned, and its culture was essentially homogeneous. In the days of Augustus himself the poet Horace had observed, with epigrammatic precision, that the Greek captive had captured its captor, Rome.[1] The standards of Hellenic culture, which the Greeks had long used to distinguish themselves from barbarians, were accepted for the most part in imperial Rome. There was no Cato to rail against the corruption of Roman morals by effeminate Greeks. If Juvenal could denounce a dirty little Greek, as he did, in the early second century, he could do no more than strike a literary pose;[2] for, even as he wrote, native speakers of Greek were holding the consulate at Rome, and

1. Hor. *Epist.* 2.1.156: *Graecia capta ferum victorem cepit.*
2. Juv. *Sat.* 3.77–78: *omnia novit / Graeculus esuriens.*

Plutarch was compiling his parallel biographies of the great
Greeks and Romans.[3]

The consolidation of the Graeco-Roman world under the
auspices of imperial Rome created a sense of security and cultural identity that had not been seen in this part of the world
since the time of the Athenian empire, more than four centuries
earlier. In that remote period (and we tend to forget just how far
away it would have seemed to the inhabitants of the Roman
empire) a Pericles or an Isocrates could proclaim in ringing
tones the unifying force of Greek culture. The παιδεία of the
Greeks distinguished them from everyone else, and everyone
else was called a barbarian. In the fragmentation of the Mediterranean world that followed the conquests of Alexander the
Great and the creation of the Hellenistic monarchies, this vision
evaporated in favor of more local nationalist ambitions—in
Macedonia, in western Asia Minor, in Syria, and in Egypt. But
once the nascent Roman state had dispatched its indigenous
enemies as well as the rival power of Carthage in North Africa,
the potent conjunction of Greece and Rome had only to await
the conclusion of the civil wars that shattered the polity of the
Roman republic.

The emergence in the Mediterranean of a coherent adminis-
trative entity that embraced the entire Graeco-Roman world
reawakened the old feelings of cultural superiority. This new
world was infinitely more diverse than the Athenian empire had
ever been. Nonetheless, from the Rock of Gibraltar to the Euphrates, from the Rhine and Danube to the Sahara, in whatever
direction one chose to move, the Greek and Latin languages
provided a common denominator. Local deities were assimilated
to the gods of the Greeks and the Romans. Local aristocracies

3. Cf. C. P. Jones, *Plutarch and Rome.*

were absorbed into the Roman aristocracy, and platoons of tax collectors, governors, and soldiers enforced both law and order.

Yet inevitably, after unification and coherence, after assimilation and consolidation, the diversity of the empire would begin to assert itself—at first with reference to the so-called barbarians at its fringes but ultimately by affirmation of the widely differing traditions within the imperial fabric itself. Old Herodotus, five hundred years before, had chronicled the diversity of the Mediterranean world as he saw it when the Athenian empire was coming into being. Herodotus was far from being an Hellenic snob; and, if he had no compunction about using the word "barbarian," he nonetheless showed a great sympathy and curiosity for barbarians of every stripe. His reports of diverse peoples and cultures had inspired conquerors like Alexander the Great by revealing the worlds that remained to be conquered. They were of markedly less interest to Hellenistic monarchs and Roman senators, for whom consolidation and conformity were higher priorities.

The vigorous revival of interest in Herodotus in the time of the Roman empire must be related to the growing interest in breaking away from the cultural conformity introduced by Augustus.[4] The writings of Hellenistic travelers, such as Pytheas of Marseille, joined with Herodotus in opening the eyes of Greek and Roman readers to the existence and diversity of many other peoples and many other places, both inside and outside the boundaries of the empire they inhabited.[5] Like Alexander before

4. G. W. Bowersock, "Herodotus, Alexander, and Rome," *The American Scholar* 58 (1989), 407–14, and in Italian as "Erodoto, Alessandro, e Roma," with annotations that are lacking in the English version, *Rivista Storica Italiana* 100 (1988; published 1989), 724–38.

5. Basic material in M. Mollat du Jourdin and J. Desanges, *Les routes millénaires* (1988), pp. 13–137 ("L'Antiquité," by Desanges).

him, the expansionist emperor Trajan could even be incited to conquest by the enticing prospect of incorporating new peoples into the empire, and it may be no accident that the greatest surviving Greek historian of Alexander was a younger contemporary of Trajan.[6] Everywhere new horizons were opening up. The alien and the exotic provided a refreshing perspective on the Hellenic standard to which the Graeco-Roman world had grown accustomed.

Fiction was obviously well suited to provide gratification for this burgeoning interest in other peoples and places. Fantastic fiction, such as we find in Lucian's *True Stories*, shows by its extreme distortions the kinds of topics that interested readers: travel into remote and unfamiliar territories (in Lucian's case the sky, the moon, and the underworld, for example), peculiar social and sexual traditions (in Lucian a society with no women in it or sexual congress without the conventional orifices), and creatures of the most diverse sizes and shapes (in Lucian, ants two hundred feet long, borrowed from Herodotus, or men who were part human and part horse).[7]

Lucian's homage to Herodotus and other earlier writers of exotica should not be taken as an end in itself. Too many modern commentators seem to feel that they have done all the work that needs to be done when they find a literary parallel. The scholar who can annotate Lucian's *True Stories* or other highly allusive works of the imperial age with a display of parallels from earlier literature will no doubt go to bed at night with the comforting conviction that nothing more needs to be done. But such a commentator is like A. E. Housman's notorious lexicographer, who, unaware that he had missed the first instance of the Latin

6. See P. A. Stadter, *Arrian of Nicomedia* (1980).

7. Lucian, *Vera Hist.* 1.22 (no women), 23 (unconventional orifices); 1.16 (ants; cf. Herod. 3.102), 18 (human and horse).

word for "cat" in compiling entries for the letter A, retired to his bed, thinking to himself, "Well done, thou good and faithful servant."[8] The question to be asked is why these literary antecedents are of such importance for the new writers of fiction. After all, one could have had domestic fiction—a kind of prose extension of the New Comedy. But one will look in vain for a Menandrian novel: it simply didn't happen in classical antiquity. Imperial fiction has a very special character. It is concerned with outsiders, with going away from home (or being wrenched away), and with brutal or occasionally agreeable confrontation with the unknown.

Greeks and Romans long had had a notorious taste for freaks. In the time of Augustus a boy with no arms ("a living herm") was put prominently on display, and some kind of fakir from India burned himself up in Athens, to the great interest of everyone around.[9] There was a lively traffic in bizarre animals, such as ostriches and giraffes.[10] The element of the circus in popular taste undoubtedly had some bearing on the turn that satire took in the early imperial period, but this was only because of a more significant development that we have already observed—the change

8. A. E. Housman, *The Confines of Criticism: The Cambridge Inaugural 1911,* ed. J. Carter (1969), pp. 42–43. Housman reproduced this passage in the preface to the corrected reprint of his edition of Juvenal (1931), pp. lv–lvi: "Everyone can figure to himself the mild inward glow of pleasure and pride which the author of this unlucky article felt while he was writing it; and the peace of mind with which he said to himself, when he went to bed that night, 'Well done, thou good and faithful servant.' This is the felicity of the house of bondage."

9. Strabo, pp. 719 (the living herm), 719–20 (the Indian Zamarus; cf. Cass. Dio 54.9.9–10).

10. For a memorable illustration of this taste, observe the eyewitness accounts of Commodus's killing an ostrich in public: Cass. Dio 73.21.1–2, Herodian 1.15.4–5.

of taste from New Comedy to Old Comedy. This change can be assigned quite precisely to the reign of Nero; for even though Horace was aware of the roots of his own satire in Aristophanes, Eupolis, and Cratinus, he certainly did not write satire in that vein. By contrast, the Neronian epigrammatist Lucillius did. His epigrams constitute a dramatic turning point in the imaginative literature of antiquity. Writing in Greek for a philhellenic emperor, this poet (in all probability a Roman) reopened the Aristophanic vein of fantasy and outrageousness.[11]

Not since Aristophanes' hero Trygaeus, in the *Peace,* had flown to heaven on the back of a dung beetle had there been anything like the epigrams of Lucillius. These epigrams not only look forward to the nonsense of Lucian's fiction: they also look sideways to the fiction of one of his own contemporary writers, Petronius, author of the one comic novel we possess, the *Satyricon.* Lucillius's poems on assorted human oddities are so bizarre, so utterly fantastic, that one would be inclined to describe them in modern terms as surrealistic. Timomachus was so tall that his house was five miles long to accommodate him when he lay on the floor. When he stood up, his slaves had to bore a hole in the roof.[12] The tiny Hermogenes was so short that, when he dropped something, he had to pull it back down to himself with a pitchfork.[13] Marcus the Thin Man once made a hole with his head in one of Epicurus's atoms and went through the middle of it.[14] The same Marcus on another occasion tried to blow a trumpet but unfortunately went headfirst right into it.[15] When thin little Proclus was fanning the fire, the smoke caught him up

11. On the Neronian background, see Chapter I above.
12. *Anth. Pal.* 11.87.
13. *Ibid.* 11.89.
14. *Ibid.* 11.93.
15. *Ibid.* 11.94.

and carried him through the window. He swam to a cloud and came down through it, wounded in a thousand places by the atoms.[16]

This gallery of bizarre characters from Lucillius provides a cultural commentary on the odd people whom we meet in Petronius's *Satyricon*—the voyeuristic Quartilla, matching sexual partners according to their size; the egregiously bad poet Eumolpus, who prescribed in his will that his legatees eat his body; to say nothing of Trimalchio and all the oddballs that populate his banquet. Few writers have ever pandered to the exotic so brilliantly as these two writers. The tastes of the emperor they served must have had something to do with it; but Nero's personal tastes would have been no more than a passing eccentricity if they had not found an echo among readers in subsequent years. This kind of writing broke the banality of the Augustan peace and challenged both the traditional Greek παιδεία and the Roman *mos maiorum*.

While Martial, writing in Latin, carried on the tradition of satiric epigram established by Lucillius, a Greek writer of fiction developed the exploration of alien and exotic peoples in a new manner, altogether different from that of Petronius. It seems that at the very time that Ptolemy Chennus ("the Quail") was fabricating his fictions about the legendary past, a certain Antonius Diogenes was writing his long and discursive novel *The Wonders beyond Thule*.[17] This work, with its obvious roots in Hellenistic travelers' tales, introduces a complicated romantic plot that links the work closely to the erotic fiction of the extant novelists from antiquity. The mechanism by which the author secures a bogus

16. *Ibid.* 11.99.
17. Photius, *Biblioth.* 109a–112a [166], pp. 140–49 (Henry); also M. Fusillo, ed., *Antonio Diogene: Le incredibili avventure al di là di Tule* (Palermo, 1990).

authenticity for his story is nothing less than the discovery of an ancient text in a grave from the time of Alexander the Great. Such a miraculous discovery of a long-lost text at a time so close to the reign of Nero cannot but remind the reader of the similar mechanism justifying the pre-Homeric account of the Trojan War in the work ascribed to Dictys of Crete.[18]

In Diogenes' tale the principal narrator, Deinias, goes across Pontus into the area of the Caspian and from there out into the reaches of Scythia and beyond. For Scythia as a land of alien peoples and customs, Herodotus was again the great model, but the question to be asked here is why Antonius Diogenes found the Herodotean model so compelling at the end of the first century. The answer undoubtedly lies in the growing tendency to break free of the Hellenic homogenization of the Roman peace in the East. Interest in Scythia in particular has a precise historical explanation. During the reign of Domitian in the eighties and nineties of the first century, Roman troops had come into direct contact with the peoples of the Danube and beyond along the edges of the Black Sea. The Suebians, the Sarmatians, and the Rhoxolani were no longer merely names to them. Beyond the eastern shore of the Black Sea there were Roman troops stationed as far as Baku on the Caspian in this period.[19] Scythia had, in short, a contemporary relevance.

18. See the remarks above near the end of Chapter I. Further, J. R. Morgan, "Lucian's *True Histories* and the *Wonders beyond Thule* of Antonius Diogenes," *CQ* 35 (1985), 475–90, esp. 481: "The discovery of books in graves was indeed a well worn ploy in ancient forgery," with citation of Dictys, Dares, and other texts. Cf. also W. Speyer, *Bücherfunde in der Glaubenswerbung der Antike*, Hypomnemata 24 (1970), pp. 43–124.

19. *Vestnik Drevnei Istorii* 1950, 177–78; *Epigraphica* 16 (1954), 118–20.

When Photius the patriarch read Diogenes' *Wonders beyond Thule*, he judged that the work was among the earliest of the fictional works in his library.[20] And he assumed, quite wrongly (as has recently been demonstrated), that Lucian's *True Stories* were deeply indebted to Antonius Diogenes.[21] Lucian's work is simply and independently a development from the same Neronian beginnings as Diogenes' own. On the other hand, the combination of remote and fantastic travel with a romantic plot and the alleged conservation of it in a long-hidden grave conspire to suggest that this reflects the new-found interest in fiction and marvels in the later first century.

Photius provides a tantalizing reference to a letter from Antonius Diogenes to a certain Faustinus about the composition of his work on the wonders beyond Thule.[22] We may conceivably have here some additional support for the placement of the novel in the time of Domitian or a little later. One of the poet Martial's principal patrons was a wealthy man by the name of Faustinus, who possessed comfortable villas at Baiae, Tivoli, and elsewhere.[23] It is clear from Martial's many allusions to him that this Faustinus was himself a man of letters and,

---

20. Photius, *Biblioth.* 111b [166], p. 148 (Henry): Ἔστι δ᾽, ὡς ἔοικεν, οὗτος χρόνῳ πρεσβύτερος τῶν τὰ τοιαῦτα ἐσπουδακότων διαπλάσαι, οἷον Λουκιανοῦ, Λουκίου, Ἰαμβλίχου, Ἀχιλλέως Τατίου, Ἡλιοδώρου τε καὶ Δαμασκίου.

21. Ibid., continuing on directly from the line quoted: Καὶ γὰρ τοῦ περὶ ἀληθῶν διηγημάτων Λουκιανοῦ καὶ τοῦ περὶ μεταμορφώσεων Λουκίου πηγὴ καὶ ῥίζα ἔοικεν εἶναι τοῦτο. For a powerful repudiation of this conjecture, see now Morgan (n. 18 above).

22. Photius, *Biblioth.* 111a [166], p. 147, ll. 32–33 (Henry): γράφει Φαυστίνῳ ὅτι τε συντάττει περὶ τῶν ὑπὲρ Θούλην ἀπίστων. . . .

23. *PIR*², F 127. Martial dedicated Books 3 and 4 of his *Epigrams* to this man.

above all, a patron of writers of all kinds. Martial's use of Greek in his epigrams makes it plain that he expected Faustinus (and others, for that matter) to be in control of that language. As Donald Russell has recently emphasized, bilingualism must have been relatively common among the literate public of the time.[24] If we take into account Faustinus's literary and antiquarian interests and his association with Martial, who was the great heir of Lucillius, this Faustinus could well be none other than the patron to Antonius Diogenes. The name is not rare, but the novelist and the epigrammatist would have had much in common. Faustinus would provide an attractive link between them.

When Diogenes' hero Deinias sets forth to the Caspian area, he evidently begins his journey from his home city (πατρίς) somewhere in western Asia Minor. He is said to have traveled across Pontus and then up into the territory between the Black Sea and the Caspian.[25] This slight indication, together with the actual name of Antonius Diogenes, may give us a hint as to the homeland of the writer. Antonius Diogenes is not a widely attested name, although the two elements of it are individually very common. The man who bore it seems to have been a Roman citizen of Greek origin. The names Antonius and Diogenes suggest this. The conjunction of this *nomen* and *cognomen* occurs in only one place in the whole of the Roman empire on present evidence, and that is the city of Aphrodisias in the province of Asia. One of the priests in that city and clearly one of its most affluent and influential citizens in the Severan period,

24. D. A. Russell, "Introduction," in *Antonine Literature* (1990), pp. 1–17.
25. Photius, *Biblioth.* 109a [166], pp. 140–41, ll. 14–16 (Henry): ἀποπλανηθεὶς τῆς πατρίδος, καὶ διὰ τοῦ Πόντου καὶ ἀπὸ τῆς κατὰ Κασπίαν καὶ Ὑρκανίαν θαλάσσης.

that is to say, about a century after the novelist, was a certain Lucius Antonius Claudius Dometinus Diogenes.[26] No one hitherto has ever thought to connect this man's family with Antonius Diogenes the writer, but there is now some reason to do so. A new and still unpublished inscription on a sarcophagus, discovered in 1990 at Aphrodisias, records other names that point to the same family: these include a Flavius Antonius Diogenes.[27] Since it has long been evident that the priest Dometinus Diogenes represented the union of two families, one with the name Antonius and the other Claudius, we are now in a position to see, through Flavius Antonius Diogenes, the branch that bore the name Diogenes. The additional nomen Flavius points directly to the latter part of the first century as a time when this family achieved recognition and citizenship. If by this argument Antonius Diogenes the novelist could be assigned to the city of Aphrodisias, it would not be without interest for the historical evolution of fiction in the eastern empire. One of the greatest of the extant Greek novelists, Chariton, certainly came from Aphrodisias, as he states explicitly at the beginning of his work.

As the excavations of Aphrodisias over the last thirty years have amply shown, it was a city of extraordinary beauty and sophistication, imbued with Hellenic culture and richly favored by the Roman government. Situated as it was in Asia Minor, where Hellenism itself was joined to ancient indigenous traditions as well as remnants of the long period of Persian rule, Aphrodisias knew what other peoples were like.[28] An inscription uncovered fifteen years ago shows that the city itself had a large

26. PIR^2, C 853.

27. The sarcophagus and its inscription will be published jointly by C. P. Jones and R. R. R. Smith in *Archäologischer Anzeiger* 1994, Heft 3.

28. Cf. K. T. Erim, *Aphrodisias, City of Venus Aphrodite* (1986).

community of Jews.[29] There is every reason to believe that a place like this could have readily inspired a narrative of cultural exotica. Perhaps more significant is the shrine of Aphrodite itself at Aphrodisias, since both Antonius Diogenes and Chariton place great emphasis on the role of this goddess in the romantic plots that they develop. Although most of what we know of Antonius Diogenes comes through the patriarch Photius and consists of a plot summary, fortunately with Chariton we are in a position to read the actual work. Like Antonius Diogenes, Chariton sets his tale in the historical past—in this case in the late fifth century B.C.—but, unlike Diogenes, Chariton places his characters entirely within the real world of the Mediterranean and the Persian kingdom.

The date of Chariton's novel, *Chaereas and Callirhoe,* is not immediately obvious, but the fortunate discovery of fragments of the novel on papyrus from the second century A.D. strongly suggests that this may be the earliest of the complete extant novels that we possess from antiquity. The relatively uncomplicated Greek style of Chariton is free from the rhetorical flamboyance of some other writers. Although this is a treacherous criterion on which to base a date, it would suggest that the novel had not been recently written at the date of the papyrus fragments, but rather that the fragments imply its popularity. At any rate, most scholars who have examined these matters would probably agree that Chariton belongs toward the end of the first century A.D. or perhaps a little later.[30] This would make him an

29. J. Reynolds and R. Tannenbaum, *Jews and Godfearers at Aphrodisias* (1987).

30. Cf. recently C. Ruiz-Montero, "Aspects of the Vocabulary of Chariton of Aphrodisias," *CQ* 41 (1991), 484–89. See also B. P. Reardon in *Collected Ancient Greek Novels* (1989), pp. 17–21; and C. P.

approximate contemporary of Antonius Diogenes. If, in fact, they both came from the same city in Asia Minor, that item would join an already substantial record of literary production from western Anatolia at this time in both prose and verse.

Since the production of fiction belongs to history, it is worth looking at one largely unremarked characteristic of Chariton's novel, because it is a characteristic that occurs nowhere else in the extant novels. Whether it was present in Antonius Diogenes we shall never know, unless papyri restore his work to us. But from beginning to end Chariton lays great stress on the cultural superiority of the Greeks. His star-crossed lovers, Chaereas and Callirhoe, pass through a bewildering series of estrangements and humiliations, all geographically located between Sicily, where the story begins, and Persia, where it reaches its dénouement. The invocation of a Hellenic standard points up the chasm between civilization and barbarism. The world of Greek culture is very much the same world as that of the fifth century B.C., so that these references to Hellenism and barbarism might possibly be explained as a part of the historical background. But no reader in the Graeco-Roman empire of the late first or second century of our era would have been able to read these passages without an identification with the shared Greek culture of that time.

Upon her arrival in Miletus after having been abducted from her tomb (where she had been placed in error in an episode reminiscent of Romeo and Juliet), Callirhoe addresses a rich man of Miletus with the words, "You are Greek, you live in a humane community, you are a civilized man—please don't be like the

---

Jones, "La personnalité de Chariton," in *Le monde du roman grec,* ed. M.-F. Baslez et al. (1992), pp. 161–67.

tomb robbers."³¹ Subsequently Chariton brings in explicit references to Greek law, Greek clothes, Greek fashion, and the behavior of Greek women.³² All this occurs in a carefully worked-out counterpoint with barbarous customs, such as those of the brutal robbers or of the Persians. Greeks are contrasted with slaves and eunuchs, and barbarians are said, strikingly, to be characterized by their inordinate respect for the king: "They think he is a god among mankind."³³ Since that particular delusion had permeated the Greeks themselves from the fifth century B.C. through the Hellenistic period and on into the Roman empire, this taunt leveled at the Persians is very probably a reflection of the skepticism of Greek intellectuals of Chariton's own day on the habit that Tacitus characterized so scathingly as "Greek adulation" (*Graeca adulatio*).³⁴

In any case, the Hellenic standard is very obvious in Chariton. It implies a society in which other peoples and other places are certainly considered inferior to the ruling peoples and places. Yet Chariton's work is unusual in this respect. The Hellenic standard may well be another indication of its early date. The momentum of imperial fiction was clearly toward sympathetic, sometimes morbidly curious description of what was alien to the Graeco-Roman world. Nothing in Photius suggests that Antonius Diogenes applied the Hellenic standard, although we cannot be sure.

31. Chariton, *Chaer. and Call.* 2.5.11.

32. *Ibid.* 3.2.2 (κατὰ νόμους Ἑλληνικούς), 4.3.7 (χλαμύδας Ἑλληνικάς), 5.4.7 (Ἑλληνικῷ σχήματι), 4.5.4 (περιεργίας Ἑλληνικῆς), 5.2.6 (φύσει δέ ἐστι τὸ βάρβαρον γυναιμανές).

33. *Ibid.* 6.7.12 (θεὸν φανερὸν νομίζουσι τὸν βασιλέα).

34. Tac. *Ann.* 6.18; see G. W. Bowersock, "Greek Intellectuals and the Imperial Cult in the Second Century A.D.," in *Le culte des souverains*, Entretiens sur l'Antiquité Classique 19 (1973), pp. 179–212.

When Deinias went from Greek Asia into Scythia, we do not know what he thought of life there. Herodotus had, after all, reported that the Scythians were in the habit of eating their relatives, and this item was far too interesting for Lucian to ignore later. Diogenes may have had something to say about it too. The *Phoenician History* of Philo of Byblos was roughly contemporary with the novels of Diogenes and Chariton. It belonged, as we have seen, to the revisionist movement that produced several invented accounts of pre-Homeric history between the reigns of Nero and Hadrian. Philo boasted that he was translating the long-lost chronicle of one Sanchuniathon, a Semite whose text showed the Greeks to be wrong on numerous points of ancient history.[35] Yet, amazingly enough, Sanchuniathon appears to have talked about the Phoenicians as barbarians (βάρβαροι).[36] Philo of Byblos was obviously unable to free himself of an ingrained habit of speech even when conjuring up an author who is supposed to have written before the Trojan War.

---

35. *FGH* III.C.790, F 1, 28. Cf. L. Troiani, *L'opera storiographica di Filone da Byblos* (1974), pp. 24–25.

36. *FGH* III.C.790, F 1, 29: οἱ παλαίτατοι τῶν βαρβάρων, ἐξαιρέτως δὲ Φοίνικές τε καὶ Αἰγύπτιοι. Cf. Troiani (n. 35 above), p. 27: "Il nostro autore qui si esprime perfettamente come un greco: egli infatti chiama 'barbari' tutti i non Greci, seguendo la tradizionale denominazione del mondo greco, per cui appunto tutti i non Greci venivano chiamati 'barbari.'" For the more substantive problem of whether Philo had access to early Near Eastern traditions that he could have ascribed to Sanchuniathon, see, e.g., O. Eissfeldt, *Sanchunjaton von Berut und Ilumilku von Ugarit* (Halle, 1952), as well as Troiani, pp. 57–77 (who doubts that Porphyry's account of Sanchuniathon can derive from another source than Philo). See also F. Millar, *The Roman Near East* (1993), p. 278: Philo's claim about Sanchuniathon "must be wholly misleading."

The Phoenician barbarians are quite enough, on their own, to impugn the credibility of Philo's claim to be translating an old Semitic chronicle.

It is Lucian to whom we must turn for a reflection of the great change in attitude toward the Hellenic standard. In a reprise of Diogenes but in a totally different key, Lucian explores the customs of the Scythians. In his dialogue entitled *Toxaris,* named for a Scythian interlocutor, Lucian presents a Greek and a Scythian in lively dialogue about their respective cultures. The main topic is friendship. The speakers are made to illustrate its importance in their respective cultures by each providing five fictional stories on this subject. The stories themselves have sufficiently novelistic and, on occasion, romantic elements that a connection between the *Toxaris* and the novel literature of the time has long been inferred.[37] But what is more notable, in comparison with the novel by Chariton, is the complete refutation of the Hellenic standard that is represented by the *Toxaris* as a whole. At one point Toxaris is made to say to the Greek Mnesippus, "Listen then, you amazing fellow, and learn how much more generously than you Greeks we barbarians judge good men."[38] Perhaps this is not such a surprise, since even Chariton could allow a character, accused before the Persian king, to praise the king's love of truth in comparison with the slanders of a clever Greek.[39] But what is more surprising is that the Greek Mnesippus in the end accepts the idea that the Scythians have a culture just as advanced and civilized as the Greeks. Mnesippus declares, "This conversation of ours and the simi-

37. Cf. C. P. Jones, *Culture and Society in Lucian* (1986), pp. 56–58.

38. Lucian, *Tox.* 5.

39. Chariton, *Chaer. and Call.* 5.7.1: ἄνθρωπος Ἕλλην, πανούργως συνθεὶς κατ᾽ ἐμοῦ ψευδεῖς διαβολάς.

larity of what we strive for [τὸ τῶν ὁμοίων ὀρέγεσθαι] are far greater guarantees" than various formal rituals such as drinking cups of blood and the other somewhat surprising things that the Scythians do.⁴⁰ The dialogue ends in a small orgy of good will and mutual respect. The atmosphere is totally removed from the world of Chariton, even though the stories told by the two speakers reflect the literary tastes of which Chariton is a prime example.

We have more than the opening of the *Wonders beyond Thule* to support the idea, first put forward by Rostovtzeff, that Lucian's *Toxaris* reflects romantic fiction with a Scythian setting.⁴¹ A papyrus fragment of the second century A.D., and therefore roughly contemporary with Lucian, preserves excerpts from a story concerning a heroine in distress by the name of Calligone.⁴² Another character bears the name Eubiotus, a curious name that also appears in one of the stories of Lucian's *Toxaris*. Eubiotus, it seems, has sent everyone out from Calligone's tent because she has had bad news about the Sarmatians, whose presence here suggests the Scythian background. We are then treated to a dramatic moment in which Calligone, in her grief and misfortune, attempts to stab herself, only to discover that Eubiotus had removed her dagger from its sheath. With operatic bravura she cries out to him, "Wickedest of men, you dared to lay your hand on my sword! I am no Amazon, no Themisto [a noted child murderess]. I am a Greek woman; I am Calligone."

The heroine's proud affirmation of her Greekness strongly echoes Chariton's harping on Hellenism as a sign of civilization

40. Lucian, *Tox.* 63.
41. M. I. Rostovtzeff, *Skythien und der Bosporos* (1931), pp. 96–99.
42. *PSI* 8.981, translated by B. P. Reardon (n. 30 above), pp. 826–27.

among barbarians. The Scythian romance on papyrus reflects a comparable sense of cultural superiority, whereas Lucian's *Toxaris* is at pains to wipe out that very sense of superiority. For Lucian, from the more or less barbarous city of Samosata on the Euphrates, civilization and dignity could be found on either side of the Roman frontier. The author of the work into which we have such a tantalizing glimpse through the accidental survival of a papyrus would seem to be on present evidence the last writer of fiction seriously to oppose Hellenism to barbarism.

If Lucian's *Toxaris* is a good representative of the toleration of diverse cultures and international diversity that characterize virtually all the extant fiction of the second century and later, other fictional forms, such as the dialogue composed by Philostratus under the name of *Heroikos,* show the same kind of cultural sympathies.[43] In the *Heroikos* an itinerant Phoenician runs across a vineyard worker on the west coast of Asia Minor and has an amiable discussion about the Homeric heroes. Both are interested in this mythological past, and both preserve their own separate national identities in examining it. Something similar occurs in the treatise on fate from the early third century of the Christian era assigned to the Syriac writer Bardaiṣan. This is the work known as *The Book of the Laws of Countries.*

Bardaiṣan, the Christian sage of Edessa, is presented in conversation with his pupils at some date in the late second or early third century.[44] The dialogue, cast clearly in the form of a Platonic dialogue (with an opening startlingly reminiscent of the opening of Plato's *Republic*), treats the topic of fate in a suspiciously pagan way that gave considerable trouble to Christian

43. See the forthcoming translation and commentary by J. Rusten.
44. For a valuable discussion of Bardaiṣan, his writings, and his time, see now J. Teixidor, *Bardesane d'Édesse: La première philosophie syriaque* (1992).

exegetes, such as Ephraem the Syrian, in subsequent centuries. The work, with its Hellenic form and pagan perspectives, citing both Chaldaean and Eygptian sources, is a good indicator of intellectual discourse in the Near East of the period. It confirms the impression one draws from the novels of a wide-ranging curiosity about alien customs and peoples and an exceptional tolerance of them. Here is Bardaişan to his pupils: "Try to understand that not all people over the whole world do that which the stars determine by their fate and in their sectors in the same way. For men have established laws in each country by that liberty given them from God, for this gift counteracts the fate of the rulers, who have appropriated something not given to them. I shall now begin to relate these, insofar as I remember them, beginning in the extreme east of the whole world."[45] With that Bardaişan reports the more bizarre customs of the Chinese: they have laws that prohibit murder, fornication, and the worship of idols. Even so, says Bardaişan ruefully, there are rich and poor people there, sick and healthy, rulers and subjects. He moves on to the Brahmans in India, among whom killing, fornication, and the worship of idols are permitted, to say nothing of the grisly habit of "eating human flesh, as other peoples eat the flesh of animals."[46]

Moving ever westward Bardaişan takes up the customs of the Persians, Medes, Bactrians, and ultimately reaches his home territory with the Edessenes and Arabs. At Hatra, we learn, anyone who steals a trifle—water, for example—is punished by stoning. Finally Bardaişan comments on the northern peoples, especially in the territory of Germany. His account of the cus-

45. Bardaişan, *Liber Legum Regionum,* 2ième tirage, ed. F. Nau (Paris, 1931), p. 19, ll. 8–16. The translation is by H. J. W. Drijvers, *The Book of the Laws of Countries* (Assen, 1964).
46. Bardaişan, *op. cit.* (n. 45), p. 20, ll. 13–15.

toms there sounds like an excerpt from Petronius's *Satyricon:*
"The boys who are handsome serve the men as wives, and a
wedding feast too is held then. This is not considered shameful
or a matter of contumely by them, because of the law obtaining
among them."⁴⁷ Summing up, Bardaiṣan gives eloquent expression to what we might call today a doctrine of cultural pluralism.
"In all places, every day in each hour," declares Bardaiṣan,
"people are born with different nativities, but the laws of men
are stronger than fate, and they lead their lives according to their
own customs. Fate does not force the Chinese to commit murder
if they do not want to, nor the Brahmans to eat meat; it does not
prevent the Persians from marrying their daughters and sisters,
the Hindus from being cremated, the Medes from being eaten by
dogs, the Parthians from marrying many wives . . . , the Gallic
men from having sexual intercourse with one another, nor the
Amazons from bringing up their little boys. . . . In each country
and each nation people use the liberty belonging to their nature
as they please."⁴⁸ The fiction that was widely read in the period
in which Bardaiṣan spoke and his pupils recorded his words (or
perhaps paraphrased them) demonstrates that his opinions were
characteristic of their age.

This pluralist and multicultural perspective is nowhere more
conspicuous than in the latest of the extant novels, the *Aethiopica*
by a certain Heliodorus. His vast and extraordinarily vivid romance belongs, in my view, securely in the later part of the fourth
century—roughly in the time of Julian the Apostate or perhaps
even a little later. Despite recent arguments to the contrary,
Heliodorus's adroit exploitation of the historical circumstances
of the siege of Nisibis by the Persians in the year 350 establishes

47. *Ibid.* p. 23, ll. 7–10.
48. *Ibid.* p. 25, ll. 8–25.

a firm *terminus post quem* for the novel. As is well known, Heliodorus's description of the siege parallels in substance and language an account of the siege of Nisibis given by Julian himself in one of his panegyrics of the emperor Constantius. Recent attempts to show that Julian's description must imitate Heliodorus, rather than the reverse, cannot stand.[49] It is clear, when Julian's words are compared with the original Syriac text of the report of the siege by Ephraem the Syrian, who was an eyewitness, that the emperor's account is reliable and not, as has been suggested on the insubstantial basis of a Latin translation of Ephraem, deviant and derivative.

In any case, there are other and much more interesting signs that Heliodorus represents a relatively late stage in Greek romantic fiction. Above all, we see the traditional opposition of Greek and barbarian brilliantly turned upside down in the *Aethiopica*. The heroine, Chariclea, is presented as a paradigm of Greek womanhood when the work opens. In the first book she herself is even made to declare to her beloved Theagenes, "It would be quite absurd if you really thought that I preferred a barbarian to a Greek."[50] Over and over again, Chariclea is admired as a Greek by most of the other characters in the story, but it turns out that she is really a fair-skinned Ethiopian. Her virtues are those of the Ethiopians. The old Calasiris similarly appears as a Greek both in dress and in culture: in Book 4 he is described as "a man who is wise, a Greek, and . . . a favorite of the gods."[51] But he is an Egyptian through and through. The interchangeability of Greek and non-Greek is symbolized at the end of the novel by the jubilant celebration of the formerly

49. See Appendix B below on the *Aethiopica*.
50. Heliod. *Aeth.* 1.25.5.
51. *Ibid.* 4.16.9.

archetypal Greek couple, Theagenes and Charicleia. On this occasion the principals give up talking Greek and speak Ethiopic "for the whole assembly to understand."[52]

Let us also look at Heliodorus's treatment of the kingdom of Aksum in Ethiopia. The historical context of the novel is apparently the sixth century B.C. Yet we find the king in Nubia, ruling over his kingdom known from its principal city of Meroe as the Meroitic kingdom, in contact with another great monarch to the south. This is explicitly the king of Aksum in Ethiopia. Now it is clear from coins as well as from inscriptions copied in antiquity that the Aksumite kingdom did not emerge into prominence until the latter part of the third century of the Christian era.[53] By that time the kingdom of Meroe was in decline. By the fourth century Aksum became the principal power in this part of Africa. The role accorded to Aksum in the *Aethiopica* of Heliodorus is accordingly a clear reflection of contemporary conditions, despite the historical setting. In a much-neglected note, published as long ago as 1919, a distinguished Italian Ethiopic scholar, Carlo Conti Rossini, called attention to the historicity of the presentation of Aksum for the lifetime of the novelist.[54] What we find there could not have been written before the end of the third century at the earliest.

The eighteenth-century English novelist Richardson composed his famous fiction *Clarissa* in the form of a series of letters. He wrote that he wished to maintain the appearance that the letters were real not because he wanted them actually to be "thought genuine," but rather in order "to avoid hurting

---

52. *Ibid.* 10.39.1 (οὐχ ἑλληνίζων ἀλλ ὥστε καὶ πάντας ἐπαίειν αἰθιοπίζων); cf. 40.1.

53. For the details of this argument, see Appendix B below.

54. C. Conti Rossini, "Meroe ed Aksum nel romanzo di Eliodoro," *Rivista degli Studi Orientali* 8 (1919/20), 233–39.

that kind of Historical Faith, which Fiction itself is genuinely read with, tho' we know it to be Fiction."[55] Rarely has the interrelation of fiction and history been stated so succinctly and so lucidly, and in this case by an acknowledged master of the craft.

In reading fiction we must be able to accept the historical context, even though we know it is not real. It must fall within the boundaries of the possible and represent what for the reader would be credible. That is why Sextus Empiricus described fictions (πλάσματα) as describing things that resemble what really happens. Julian obviously understood this too when he denounced πλάσματα that were created in the form of history. Near the end of his life, in his rage against the city of Antioch, he was able to turn this understanding to powerful effect by writing a piece of satiric fiction himself. His *Caesars*—a savage review of the emperors of Rome, culminating with a licentious Constantine in the grip of Christianity—is as securely anchored in the fourth century as the dialogues of Lucian, to which it is indebted, were anchored in the second.

Among the most memorable of exotic folk in the Greek romances are the robbers in the Nile Delta who appear under the name of Boukoloi, "cowherds" or, as Winkler adroitly named them, "desperadoes" or "rangers." They first appear, in the extant literature, in Achilles Tatius and, very probably about the same time, in the Phoenician novel ascribed to a Lollianus, of which fragments survive on papyrus.[56] These bold and savage

55. Cited by F. Kermode in his *The Genesis of Secrecy* (1979), p. 161, acknowledging that he owed the quotation to H. Frei, *The Eclipse of Biblical Narrative* (1974), p. 144.
56. Achil. Tat. *Leuc. and Clit.* 3.9, 4.7–18. "Rangers" in J. Winkler's translation in his English version of the whole work in B. P. Reardon, ed., *Collected Ancient Greek Novels.* Earlier he had used the

people were, it seems, good soldiers and cannibals—an ideal mix for fiction. They reappear later in Heliodorus's *Aethiopica*.[57]

But with the Boukoloi fiction and history clearly overlap, since the sober historian Cassius Dio also gives an account of them under the year 172, when they undertook a revolt against Roman authority in Egypt.[58] This revolt was noticed as well by the mischievous author of the *Augustan History,* who introduced *Bucolici milites*—"the soldier Bucoli"—into his biographies of both Marcus Aurelius and Avidius Cassius.[59] Their fame lasted into the fourth century, when Jerome called them *barbara tantum et ferox natio*—"a barbarous and fierce nation."[60] The notoriety of the Boukoloi in history seemed to provide a lifeline to scholars working on the novels. It was commonly, if imprudently, assumed that the revolt of 172 must have been so widely noticed that all literary references to the Boukoloi would have to reflect it.[61] Hence we are supposed to have a clear *terminus* after which Achilles Tatius and Lollianus wrote.

Fiction, however, is not like that. It reflects a historical setting, a milieu, a way of life and thought, but not normally an event. The Boukoloi did not spring out of the void in 172. Their depredations, less bold perhaps, but nonetheless memorable, must

------

term "desperadoes" in "Lollianus and the Desperadoes," *JHS* 100 (1980), 155–81. For Lollianus, see A. Henrichs, *Die Phoinikika des Lollianos* (1972), pp. 48–51.

57. Heliod. *Aeth.* 1.5–6, 2.24.1.
58. Cass. Dio 72.4.1–2.
59. *HA* Marcus 21.2, Avid. Cass. 6.7.
60. Jer. (Hieron.) *Vita Hil.* 43 (*PL* 23.52–53).
61. E.g., J. Schwartz, "Quelques observations sur des romans grecs," *AC* 36 (1967), 536–52, esp. 540–42; and Henrichs, *loc. cit.* (n. 56 above).

certainly precede that date. And now a carbonized roll from the Egyptian Delta proves this. In 166/67 they are seen to be at their deadly work. Achilles Tatius had specified a certain Nikochis as their base, and the new document confirms this by calling these brigands "the impious Neikokeitai" (οἱ ἀνόσιοι Νεικωκεῖται).[62] The historical revolt of 172 immediately loses its force as a dating criterion. The Boukoloi were there all along.

Naturally they would form part of Egyptian episodes, just as naturally as eunuchs appear in Persian scenes. These are not stock motifs, inasmuch as they mirror the real world. But at the same time they are not necessarily indicators of a recent event. What they do indicate is the absorption of writers and readers in alien customs, the emergence of new standards of otherness— not only foreignness but social marginality as well. Fiction, and perhaps fiction alone, signals the disappearance of barbarism as a conceptual means of asserting the superiority of Graeco-Roman culture. The old standard of Hellenism broke down in the second and third centuries, and in doing so it made way for a new kind of Hellenism, an ecumenical Hellenism that could actually embrace much that was formerly barbaric. Heliodorus is a memorable example of this. The Hellenism of late antiquity was, in fact, to become the voice of the barbarians as they cried out against the tide of Christianity.

---

62. *P. Thmouis* I, col. 104, l. 13, and col. 116, ll. 4–5. (I am indebted to Ann Hanson for directing me to this papyrus.) For Νίκωχις (*sic*) in Achil. Tat., see *Leuc. and Clit.* 4.12.8. In S. Kambitsis's publication of the papyrus (1985), the editor credits (p. 99) M. Manfredi with making the connection between the Νίκωχις of the Boukoloi in Achilles Tatius and the Νεικωκεῖται of the new papyrus.

CHAPTER THREE

The Wounded Savior

The eminent philosopher Dio of Prusa, known as
Chrysostom ("the Golden Mouth"), could pride himself on being
one of the leading Greek intellectuals of his time. He was per-
sonally acquainted with the emperor Trajan, who listened with
patience and incomprehension to the stream of wisdom that the
great man poured into the imperial ear. A century later the
biographer Philostratus accorded Dio Chrysostom an ample biography in his collected *Lives of the Sophists,* even though, by
Philostratus's own admission, Dio was not a sophist. Few today
would contest that Dio ranks among the truly representative
figures of the late first and early second centuries of the Christian
era. His personal opinions are always bound to be of some
interest.[1]

It so happens that, when Dio was a guest at the villa of an
evidently affluent Roman friend, he woke up one morning feeling
rather frail (for reasons he does not divulge). After rising to face
the rigors of the day, he took a few turns in a chariot in his host's
private hippodrome, oiled and washed himself, and then settled
down to read some tragedies. What he chose were three plays

1. Cf. C. P. Jones, *The Roman World of Dio Chrysostom* (1978);
and P. Desideri, *Dione di Prusa: Un intellettuale greco nell'impero
romano* (1978). For Trajan's incomprehension, see Philos. *Vit. Soph.*
p. 488.

55

about Philoctetes, one each by Aeschylus, Sophocles, and Euripides.[2] Dio indulged in the pleasing fantasy that he might be, as it were, a judge in a dramatic competition of the fifth century B.C., appraising the relative merits of these three dramas from the greatest of the classical Greek dramatic poets. That they were all on the same theme gave special point to the comparison. Unfortunately, modern readers are not in a position to repeat Dio's experiment, since the works by Aeschylus and Euripides no longer survive, although some fragments as well as the observations of Dio permit us to have a sense of what those works were like.[3] The *Philoctetes* by Sophocles does, however, survive, and it remains today perhaps the most intensely personal and moving of all Greek tragedies.

Philoctetes figures only a few times in the Homeric poems,[4] but it is clear that the later epics gave him more attention. In the fifth century B.C. the outlines of his career were obviously well known to all cultivated Greeks. The epics and plays had established him as a significant figure in the mythology that was, for the Greeks, history at the same time. Philoctetes had once gone forth with the Greek expedition to Troy after rendering a signal service to Heracles on his last day of mortality. It was Philoctetes who put the torch to the pyre on which Heracles was cremated, and in

2. Dio Prus. *Orat.* 52. Cf. M. T. Luzzatto, *Tragedia greca e cultura ellenistica: L'or. LII di Dione di Prusa* (1983).
3. See, e.g., W. M. Calder III, "Aeschylus' *Philoctetes*," *GRBS* 11 (1970), 171–79, and *id.*, "A Reconstruction of Euripides' *Philoctetes*," *Greek Numismatics and Archaeology: Essays in Honor of Margaret Thompson*, ed. O. Mørkholm and N. Waggoner (1979), pp. 53–62; and S. D. Olson, "Politics and the Lost Euripidean *Philoctetes*," *Hesperia* 60 (1991), 269–83.
4. *Iliad* 2.718; *Odyss.* 3.190, 8.219.

grateful anticipation of this selfless act Heracles had turned over to him his unerring bow. Through immolation Heracles escaped the poison of Deianira's robe and became divine.

Philoctetes acquired the bow that no enemy could avoid. He thereby became a desirable member of any military expedition, but unfortunately his relations with Odysseus were bad. That notoriously wily Greek managed to expel Philoctetes from the Greek expedition after he had been bitten by a snake while sacrificing at a shrine of Chryse on the island of Tenedos in the Aegean. The snakebite caused a wound that would not heal, and the smell, as well as the lamentations, of Philoctetes sufficed to persuade the Greeks to abandon him on the desolate island of Lemnos. There he remained for nearly the entire duration of the Trojan War. But ten years later the Greeks learned through a captured Trojan prophet that Troy could only be taken with the bow of Philoctetes and, in most versions of the story, in the presence of Philoctetes himself.[5]

This suffering pariah, abandoned by his own people and wracked by a suppurating wound that would never close, had already become in the fifth century a powerful symbol of the salvation that man by his own folly puts out of his reach and must struggle somehow to regain. The Athenians saw Sophocles' play for the first time in 409, when Alcibiades, now far away, seemed to hold the secret of restoring their fortunes after the disaster of the Sicilian expedition. For Sophocles himself Philoctetes is a man whose very loneliness and agony serve to inspire the young son of Achilles, Neoptolemos, and to transform his character. Unlike the plays of Aeschylus and Euripides, which were both written much earlier than Sophocles' work, this is essentially a

5. Still useful, over a century later, is L. A. Milani, *Il mito di Filottete nella letteratura classica e nell'arte figurata* (1879).

drama of the impact of suffering on the mind of a young man. At the beginning of the play Odysseus persuades the youth to trick Philoctetes in order to recover the bow and his person. But by befriending him and observing his excruciating pain, by hearing his ear-splitting cries and smelling the foul odors of his wound, Neoptolemos comes to realize the wrong he has committed in joining in an act of deception. He resolves, to Odysseus's horror, to turn back the bow that Philoctetes, in a moment of terrible pain, had entrusted to him because he honestly believed the boy a friend. There are few plays in which suffering holds center stage for so long as it does in Sophocles' *Philoctetes*.[6]

Presumably this was the reason that Dio Chrysostom, while admiring the language of Sophocles and the tragic power of his play, found Aeschylus and Euripides more congenial. Both were more directly concerned with the knotty political problem of abducting a savior who was unaware that he was a savior. Euripides' play, produced for the first time in 431 and obviously exuding the atmosphere of Periclean Athens, was, according to Dio, a highly political work that effectively fostered virtue (ἀρετή) in the reader. Odysseus appeared as a loyal and energetic patriot, taking on one dangerous mission after another for the common good in a spirit of public involvement that echoed Pericles' funeral oration as we know it from the pages of Thucydides. Dio liked Euripides' play so much that he not only described it in his comparative essay on the three plays; he also drafted a prose paraphrase of the whole opening scene. This survives to give us a clear picture of the characters of Odysseus and Philoctetes in Euripides.[7] The invalid exile clearly accepted

---

6. Edmund Wilson's famous essay "The Wound and the Bow," in a volume of the same title (1947), remains a rare modern example of critical appreciation of this remarkable play.

7. Dio Prus. *Orat.* 59. See Olson (n. 3 above).

the same premises of political involvement as Odysseus himself and claimed that his wound was nothing less than the result of an effort to make a sacrifice on behalf of the entire Greek army. The suffering of Philoctetes was manifestly of far less interest to Euripides than to Sophocles. At the end of Dio Chrysostom's paraphrase Philoctetes is made to observe that, although his pain had been unendurable at the start, it was now, after nine years, not so bad any more.

It is a rare privilege to be able to look at these three plays through the eyes of a leading Greek intellectual of the Roman imperial period. His fascination with the Philoctetes story is obvious. We cannot simply assume that he picked up the nearest book rolls in his host's villa on that day when he was feeling somewhat fatigued. Philoctetes, the wounded savior, meant something to Dio and to his world. By exploring the fabrications to which this classic myth was subjected over many centuries from Sophocles to Dio and beyond, we can see why. Then, as now, a pariah who embodied salvation was an irresistible paradox.

In the classical Greek world nobody was sacrosanct, certainly not the figures of mythology. We cannot be surprised to find that there are even traces of a considerable comic literature on this figure as well as several other lesser tragedies.[8] The general tenor of the comic treatment of Philoctetes is probably well represented by some unattributed verses in the writings of one of Dio Chrysostom's great contemporaries, Plutarch. A speaker is made to say, "What young maiden, what young virgin would have you, Philoctetes? You are unfortunately not marriageable."[9]

8. Comedies by Epicharmus, Strattis, and Antiphanes; tragedies by Achaeus, Philocles, and Theodectes: cf. Milani (n. 5 above), pp. 45–47.

9. Plut. *An Seni Res Publica Gerenda Sit* 9, 789A (Kock no. 1215).

But such crude lines as these simply ring changes on the familiar story.

The first truly creative invention applied to the Philoctetes legend can be observed in the third century B.C., in the relatively early Hellenistic period. Someone had the completely original idea of taking Philoctetes to Italy after the conclusion of the Trojan War. This piece of patent fiction imposed upon a quasi-historical myth introduces a shipwreck on Philoctetes' way back to Greece after the death of Paris and the Greek victory at Troy. The boat with Philoctetes ends up on the Italian coast in Campania, where he founds a number of cities, including Krimissa, Chone, and Makalla. The great savior erects a temple to Apollo, dedicates his bow to the god, and ultimately dies in combat on Italian soil. All this looks very much like an effort to coopt Philoctetes for the cause of the new Roman state.[10] After all, the Greeks had treated him badly, by leaving him on the island of Lemnos for nine years and then trying by deceit to steal both him and his bow. As the legendary descendants of the Trojans, the Romans would have had good reason to feel some sympathy for this Greek, even if his bow ultimately brought an end to their city in Asia Minor.

The story of Philoctetes in Italy appears at some length in two major verse writers whose relations to each other are regrettably impossible to establish with any certainty. But it is likely that the little epic (ἐπύλλιον) entitled *Philoctetes* by Euphorion of Chalkis was the first work to incorporate this late and last phase

---

See Martial, *Epig.* 2.84, and Auson. *Epig.* 79 for other probable traces of the comic representation of Philoctetes.

10. See the discussion of these innovations by B. A. van Groningen, *Euphorion* (1977), pp. 114–16. Cf. Milani (n. 5 above), p. 30.

of Philoctetes' career.[11] A repetition of this material in the obscure poem known as the *Alexandra* and ascribed to the Hellenistic poet Lycophron probably belongs to a somewhat later date in the third century than the poem of Euphorion.[12] There is a knotty problem here, but on present evidence we have good reason to think that Lycophron was writing in the early third century, even though the extensive account he gives of Romulus and Remus, Aeneas, and the foundation of Roman power seems wholly incompatible with such an assumption.[13] Similarly the parallel with Euphorion on the Philoctetes story contributes to disturbing a postulated early third-century date for Lycophron. Were one to imagine, as some have, that passages such as these are all interpolations in an earlier poem, one would soon discover that the *Alexandra* is more interpolation than original. That would obviously not be a satisfactory situation. But fortunately, for our purposes, the exact relation of Euphorion to Lycophron is irrelevant to the general point that Philoctetes becomes important to Roman Italy by the third century B.C.

Sometime in the following century one of Rome's greatest dramatic poets, Accius, wrote a tragedy in Latin on Philoctetes.[14] From the extant fragments it is impossible to be certain to what extent, if any, Accius was following one or another of the great

11. See van Groningen (n. 10 above), 113–14 for the remains of Euphorion's poem.

12. Lycoph. *Alex.* 911–29 (Krimissa, death in Italy, grave at Makella).

13. See G. W. Mooney, *The Alexandra of Lycophron* (London, 1921), pp. 131–37 on lines 1226–80 (on Romulus, Remus, Aeneas, and Roman power).

14. For the fragments of the *Philocteta* of Accius, see *Tragicorum Romanorum Fragmenta*, ed. O. Ribbeck (Leipzig, 1879), pp. 236–42.

Greek tragedians (or even one of the lesser ones), but there is a strong possibility that his account exploited the new Italian connection of the savior. At least one fragment might possibly evoke the shipwreck that Euphorion described in lines of his little epic that are still extant.[15] It is also likely that Accius drew at least some parts of his play from Euripides, who introduced an embassy from Troy to make the case against Odysseus in the presence of Philoctetes: one of the fragments of Accius's drama suggests that the argument between the Trojans and Odysseus was rehearsed in the Latin play.[16] But of one characteristic of Accius's treatment we can be in no doubt, for we have an extended discussion of it by Cicero in both the *Tusculan Disputations* and the *De Finibus Bonorum et Malorum (The Limits of Good and Evil).*[17] Accius clearly put Philoctetes on the stage crying out in pain as he suffered from the seizures that regularly afflicted him every time the never-closing wound began to throb, burst, and flow with blood.

Just as in Sophocles' play, the Philoctetes of Accius fills his desert island with desperate cries of pain: "Iaceo in tecto umido, / Quod eiulatu, questu, gemitu fremitibus / Resonando mutum flebilis voces refert." ("I lie in a damp abode, which echoes from its silent walls the tearful cries, with lamentation, wailing, groaning, and roaring.")[18] Cicero's discussion of Philoctetes' cries re-

15. Euphorion *apud* van Groningen (n. 10 above), p. 113; with Accius, *Philoct.* frg. 2 Ribbeck (n. 14 above).

16. Accius, *Philoct.* frg. 17 Ribbeck (n. 14 above): "Phrygiam miti more esse, animo immani Graeciam"; with which cf. Dio Prus. *Orat.* 59.4, παρὰ τῶν Φρυγῶν πρέσβεις.

17. Cicero, *Tusc. Disp.* 2.7, 19; 2.14, 32–33; *De Fin.* 2.29, 94.

18. In Ribbeck (n. 14 above) as frg. 11, cited by Cicero in *Tusc. Disp.* 2.14, 33; *De Fin.* 2.29, 94.

veals explicitly, and for the first time, a deeply rooted Roman aversion to the spectacle of uncontrolled grief, especially in a man. The Stoics would not, of course, have approved, and their view of the endurance of pain proved very congenial among the Romans. Even, it would seem, some Greeks of the classical age took a dim view of unrestrained masculine emotion. An extant fragment of Euripides' play shows that it was political activity on behalf of one's city that surely established your credentials as a man, or, as Dio put it in his paraphrase of the passage, to be "really" a man.[19] Sitting on his island of Lemnos, Philoctetes clearly did not measure up. In the *Tusculan Disputations* and the *De Finibus* Cicero was concerned to advocate self-control and the restraint of emotions. Philoctetes, and implicitly those who watched him on the stage, violated Roman decorum. In the *De Finibus* Cicero elaborated his point as follows: "There are certain precepts for courage (one might even say laws), which forbid a man to behave like a woman in grief. Accordingly we must judge disgraceful—not grief itself, for sometimes that is indeed necessary—but filling the rocks of Lemnos with the foul clamor of a Philoctetes. . . . Let us rather say: it is disgraceful, it is unmanly to be weakened by grief, to be broken by it, or to succumb to it."[20]

19. Eur. *Philoct.* frg. 788 (Nauck²): οὐδὲν γὰρ οὕτω γαῦρον ὡς ἀνὴρ ἔφυ. / τοὺς γὰρ περισσοὺς καί τι πράσσοντας πλέον / τιμῶμεν ἄνδρας τ' ἐν πόλει νομίζομεν. In Dio Prus. *Orat.* 59.1, the paraphrase is: ἀλλὰ γὰρ ἴσως χαλεπὸν εὑρεῖν οὕτω μεγαλόφρον καὶ φιλότιμον ὁτιοῦν ὡς ἀνὴρ πέφυκεν. τοὺς γὰρ φανεροὺς καὶ πλειόνων ἅπτεσθαι τολμῶντας σχεδὸν τούτους ἅπαντες θαυμάζομεν καὶ τῷ ὄντι ἄνδρας ἡγούμεθα.

20. Cicero, *De Fin.* 2.29, 94–95. The final words translated "potius ergo illa dicantur: turpe esse, viri non esse debilitari dolore, frangi, succumbere."

By the late republic, the time of Cicero, Philoctetes had become a symbol of masculine weakness, of effeminacy, of the failure of a man to endure with courage as a man. This new interpretation of Philoctetes' suffering was soon translated into learned fiction and witty epigrams. The town of Makalla, which Philoctetes was said, according to the more recent legends, to have founded in Italy, was now said to have taken its name from Philoctetes' committing effeminate acts in it. This is a word play by metathesis on μαλακισθῆναι, "to be softened; to be effeminate," and the name of the place, Makalla.[21] In the early imperial period the epigrammatist Martial turned out an epigram on Philoctetes, characterized as *mollis* or "soft."[22] Roman correctness destroyed the heroic suffering of this great figure and turned him into a target of sexual jokes. But Philoctetes was far too strong in legend to be diminished by this kind of conservative moralizing. The very point on which Cicero faulted Philoctetes, his unrestrained crying out in pain, proved more than a millennium later to be the provocation for one of the most incisive writings of modern times on ancient taste and on Philoctetes in particular.

In the eighteenth century the German critic Gotthold Ephraem Lessing rose to the defense of both Philoctetes and Sophocles against the strictures of Cicero and others like him, including Adam Smith and a long-forgotten French dramatist, Chateaubrun, of the seventeenth century. In his great treatise *Laokoön*, on the limits of painting and poetry, Lessing undertook to refute Winckelmann's view of Greek art as an expression of noble simplicity and quiet greatness ("edle Einfalt und stille Größe"). For Lessing the Laocoön statue symbolized precisely the opposite characteristic in ancient art, a willingness to show

21. Schol. *ad* Thuc. 1.12: ἀπὸ τοῦ μαλακισθῆναι ἐν αὐτῇ Φιλοκτήτην.
22. Martial, *Epig.* 2.84.

extreme emotion and not to be afraid of tears and cries of anguish. Lessing discussed Sophocles' *Philoctetes* at length in order to demonstrate the centrality of the hero's pain to a proper understanding of the work. In doing this he picked up the parallel that Winckelmann had drawn between Laocoön and Philoctetes: "Laocoön suffers," wrote Winckelmann (as quoted by Lessing), "but he suffers like Sophocles' Philoctetes. His wretchedness goes to our soul, but we would wish to be able to bear our wretchedness like this great man."[23]

Lessing emphasized the arousal of pity and sympathy at the horrifying spectacle of someone in pain, someone who did not bear suffering nobly but screamed against it. He denounced Adam Smith for considering it unseemly to display suffering and admirable to contain it. He subjected the playwright Chateaubrun to a vigorous attack for equipping Philoctetes with plenty of company on his island as well as young Neoptolemos with a wife. Lessing excoriated modern Europeans—"we Europeans, more sensitive inhabitants of a cleverer age"—because courtesy and decency forbade cries and tears.[24] For Cicero he had nothing but contempt. Of Cicero's advocacy of Stoic endurance of physical pain he wrote: "One would think that he [Cicero] wanted to train a gladiator, so zealous is he against the external expression of pain" ("Man sollte glauben, er wolle einen Gladiator abrichten, so sehr eifert er wider den äußerlichen Ausdruck des Schmerzes").[25] Lessing went on to stress the Romans' enthusiasm for gladiatorial sport: their pleasure would be impaired, he suggested, if the gladiators were to show signs of

---

23. G. E. Lessing, *Laokoön*, ed. K. Balser (1982), pp. 168–69.
24. *Ibid.* 170: "Ich weiß es, wir feinern Europäer einer klügern Nachwelt wissen über unsern Mund und über unsere Augen besser zu herrschen."
25. *Ibid.* 191.

physical pain. To this taste Lessing even ascribed the failure of Seneca's tragedies, peopled, in his view, by "pugilists in the cothurnus" ("Klopffechter im Kothurne").[26]

By the time of the Roman empire it was apparent that the Philoctetes story required further revision, and the writers of mythical fiction soon provided it. The newly fabricated history of the Trojan War, ascribed to the allegedly pre-Homeric Dictys of Crete and made known miraculously in the reign of Nero, presents a wholly sanitized Philoctetes, suitable for Romans of all ages. In the second book of his *Trojan War* Dictys presents Philoctetes as sacrificing at the temple of Apollo Smintheus in Asia Minor at the beginning of the Trojan expedition.[27] The classical legend, of course, had him at a temple of Chryse, but there is little doubt that the association of Philoctetes with the temple of Apollo in Italy must have led someone, the author of the Dictys story or someone before him, to bring Philoctetes and Apollo together at this early stage. Chryse is now metamorphosed into a priest of Apollo by the name of Chryses. Philoctetes is duly bitten by the snake, which Odysseus kills.[28] Then follows the most remarkable rewriting of the story. Philoctetes, we are told, is removed with a small band of associates to the isle of Lemnos in order to be cured. A shrine of Vulcan there was said to have priests who were particularly skilled in the healing of snakebites.[29] We may perhaps surmise that Lemnos has been assimilated in this instance with the famous healing island of Cos.

26. *Ibid.* 192.
27. Dictys Cret. 2.14.
28. *Ibid.*
29. *Ibid.*: "Neque multo post Philocteta cum paucis, uti curaretur, Lemnum insulam mittitur, namque in ea sacra Vulcano antistites dei inhabitare ab accolis dicebatur solitos mederi adversus venena huiusmodi."

This transformation of the legend has thus eliminated altogether the traditional reasons for removing Philoctetes—his cries
of pain and the odor of the wound. He is assigned companions,
and healing is the sole motivation for the Greek action. Even at
the time of the bite, according to Dictys, Odysseus is alerted to
what has happened by a clamor that is raised (*clamore sublato*),
not by the stricken Philoctetes himself but rather by the people
who were standing around and became alarmed. In other words,
Dictys's recreation of the story introduces a Philoctetes who
conforms perfectly to the Roman standard of masculinity. Nowhere in the remaining books of Dictys's work does Philoctetes
violate this norm, although the author acknowledges that his
healing did not come as rapidly as expected. He continues to be
weak (*invalidus*) and limping (*neque satis firmo gressu*, "and
with an insufficiently firm step").[30]

As far as we can tell, this sanitized portrait of Philoctetes was
introduced as a part of the Homeric revisionism in the Neronian
period. It did not go away. It echoed the moral standards of the
Graeco-Roman world of the time. The emperor Marcus Aurelius, in his *Meditations*, particularly thanked his teacher Apollonius, a Stoic philosopher from Chalcedon, for instilling in him
an indifference to pain, loss, and disease: "to maintain a similar
demeanor in every circumstance [τὸ ἀεὶ ὅμοιον]—in sharp pain,
upon the loss of a child, or in protracted illness."[31] Even Marcus's contemporary the valetudinarian sophist Aelius Aristides
subscribed to a proverb, first quoted by Alcibiades in Plato's
Symposium, that a man who has been bitten by a snake will talk
only to those who have also been bitten by a snake—for they
alone can understand him. The proverb alludes clearly to Philoc-

---

30. *Ibid.* 2.47.
31. Marcus Aur. *Ad Se Ipsum* 1.8.

tetes, as Aristides observes in one of the two places where he quotes it, and it was therefore apt for Plato to give it to Alcibiades—in view of the connection between the two figures in 409.[32] The saying suggests the futility of displaying one's feelings before anyone who cannot comprehend them. Aristides fully accepted this wisdom and poured out his heart only in the *Sacred Discourses,* to his healing god Asclepius.

A century and a half after Dictys, when the sophistic writer Philostratus composed his imaginary dialogue on ancient heroes, he presented what we might call the imperial Philoctetes in an even more dramatically improved image. In the dialogue, known as the *Heroikos,* a vine dresser in the Troad declares that he has learned the truth about Philoctetes from the long-dead Protesilaus, now resurrected and engaging in amiable discourse in the vineyards of Asia Minor. Protesilaus can assure the vineyard worker, who in turn assures his interlocutor from Phoenicia and, naturally, the readers of the *Heroikos,* of the following corrections in the story of Philoctetes.[33] First, no priest had ever prophesied that Troy could be taken only by the bow of Philoctetes and in his presence. The consequence of denying the prophecy is that Odysseus would no longer have any cause to engage in trickery to remove Philoctetes. Second, according to Protesilaus, Philoctetes was definitely not alone on the island of Lemnos: it was, as indeed both Aeschylus and Euripides had portrayed it, inhabited. Third, and very important, Philoctetes was actually cured on the island of Lemnos before he departed for Troy. Fourth, and perhaps most important, Philoctetes stoically endured his pain and never gave vent to unseemly cries of lamentation. It was the mud of Lemnos, we are told, that had a miraculous healing effect

---

32. Plato, *Symp.* 217e–218a; with Ael. Arist. *Orat.* 17.18, 28.130.
33. The account of Philoctetes is all told in chapter 5 of the *Heroikos,* pp. 171–73 (Kayser).

on Philoctetes' wound, driving out the disease and stopping the flow of blood. Hence, when the hero went to Troy, he was neither ailing (οὔτε νοσοῦντα) nor like someone who had been sick (οὔτε νενοσηκότι ὅμοιον). Inasmuch as, according to this version, the healing took place immediately upon his arrival on Lemnos, we are left to wonder what kind of a life Philoctetes passed there for the nine or so years before he returned to Troy.

The systematic elimination of the unseemly and unmanly tradition of Philoctetes' agony seems to have been accompanied, in the Roman imperial age, with philosophical reflections on the artistic representation of pain. Several references in Plutarch as well as three epigrams in the *Palatine Anthology* all make plain that there had been famous depictions of Philoctetes in both painting and sculpture. Already in the Flavian period, as Lessing was the first to observe, the Elder Pliny had made reference to a sculpture by Pythagoras of Rhegion, before which, according to Pliny, spectators themselves seemed to feel the pain of Philoctetes' wound.[34] The realistic depiction of a man in pain was, however, very different from hearing him react to that pain, either in reality or in the theater. Among the topics discussed in his table conversations, Plutarch introduced the problem, which was as old as Plato, of emotions felt upon beholding the diseased or dying. We certainly do not take any pleasure in looking at them or hearing them, but Plutarch noted rightly that we do take pleasure in the artistic representation of them.[35] It was important to recognize that what makes these representations acceptable is the distance that the artistic medium puts between the reality of

34. Pliny, *NH* 34.8 (19), 59, discussed by Lessing (n. 23 above), pp. 179–80. The Philoctetes was at Syracuse: "Syracusis autem claudicantem, cuius ulceris dolorem sentire etiam spectantes videntur." Lessing's text of Pliny assigned the sculptor to Leontini instead of Rhegion.
35. Plut. *Quaes. Conviv.* 5.1, 673C–674D.

suffering and ourselves. In other words a sculpture of Philoctetes in agony, such as that by Pythagoras of Rhegion, or a painting, such as the great one by Parrhasius, commemorated in an epigram (and mentioned by Plutarch in another passage),[36] gives us Philoctetes suffering in silence. His cries cannot be heard. That is clearly why Plutarch and others found them acceptable. Yet, as the epigrammatists bear ample witness, part of the fascination of these works of art was the closeness that the spectator felt to the real thing. You could almost feel his pain. For those with the sensibilities to accept it, you could almost hear Philoctetes cry.

For Lessing's understanding of Greek culture that posed something of a problem. He argued persuasively against Winckelmann that the audible expression of strong emotion is an integral part of Sophocles' play and that Cicero's repudiation of such expression represented later morality, introduced by the Stoics and championed by the Romans. But in terms of art—and we should remember that Lessing's treatise is on the limits of art and poetry—Winckelmann may well have been right in insisting on the silence of Laocoön in the famous sculpture. Lessing wanted to hear that terrible cry, whereas Winckelmann perceived it as no more than a sigh. The impact of the long-lost sculptures and paintings of Philoctetes must have been, in some way, rather similar to the impact of the extant Laocoön. Plutarch's observation would seem to apply to it as well as to the Philoctetes piece. We would not want to hear the cries or smell the wound, but we do appreciate looking at a magisterial representation of suffering. This is not exactly what Lessing set out to demonstrate. But then Plutarch was far closer in his outlook to Cicero than to Sophocles, and it was to Sophocles that Lessing appealed for the truly Greek point of view. In the Roman imperial age, the Sopho-

36. Plut. *De Aud. Poet.* 3, 18C–D. Cf. *Anth. Pal.* 16.111.

clean manner was, as Dio Chrysostom proves, admired but not altogether acceptable or even welcome. It was too disturbing.

It was perhaps because of this distancing of the suffering of Philoctetes that another aspect of the hero's career took on a new importance in the second century of the Christian era. He had ignited the pyre that consumed the earthly remains of Heracles and consigned that great hero to perpetual divinity. Liberation by death had a long and distinguished tradition in classical antiquity, extending back at least as far as Empedocles' leap into Mount Aetna. The Indian Brahman Calanus, in the entourage of Alexander the Great, had had himself burned alive and, it may be noted, won the admiration of Cicero two centuries later because he, like other Brahmans, was consumed by the flames *sine gemitu*—without uttering a sound.[37] But in the Roman imperial period the self-immolation of the Indian sage Zamarus in the days of Augustus was the best remembered until the spectacular demise of the philosopher Peregrinus in the year 165.[38] This eccentric philosopher and wise man, with an un-paralleled taste for the theatrical, had himself burned up before a crowd of spectators who assembled for the occasion after the Olympic games. As Lucian reports, in what is generally agreed to be a largely historical account, Peregrinus made a speech before his fiery demise. It is clear that the model of Heracles and Philoctetes was foremost in his mind: "One who has lived like Heracles should die like Heracles and be commingled with the aether. I want to help mankind by showing them the way to

---

37. Cicero, *Tusc. Disp.* 5.77 (on Indian *sapientes*); cf. 2.52 on Calanus in particular (whose death moved Cicero to observe, "apis aculeum sine clamore ferre non possumus"). Again on Calanus, Cicero, *De Div.* 1.47.

38. Zamarus: Strabo 719–20; Cass. Dio 54.9.9–10. For Peregrinus Lucian's essay is the principal document.

despise death. Therefore, everyone should become my Philoctetes" (πάντας οὖν δεῖ μοι τοὺς ἀνθρώπους Φιλοκτήτας
γενέσθαι).³⁹

Here Peregrinus casts himself in the role of a helper of mankind, but it is only through the agency of Philoctetes that he can
enact the salvation and divinization of his patron, Heracles.
There is certainly an element of mockery when Lucian reports
that Peregrinus urged all people to join in burning him up by all
becoming Philocteteses, but the emphasis on divinity through
death is very striking. Peregrinus sees himself as helping to de-
stroy the fear of death. He does this by rejoicing in his self-
destruction. There is no lamentation or wailing here, only ex-
altation and the injunction for others to do likewise. But he needs
a Philoctetes—or rather many Philocteteses—to achieve his
goal. Philoctetes' role in liberating Heracles through death
showed him as a savior even before he became the savior of Troy.
Heracles bequeathed him the bow for his service, and this naturally strengthened the Greek expedition at the beginning as well
as saved it at the end.

In this way the second century enriched the soteriology of the
Philoctetes story. But it did so by drawing out implications that
Dio Chrysostom had already seen in the Euripidean (and for the
Roman world the most accessible) version of the story in classic
tragedy. As we have seen, both Odysseus and Philoctetes represented themselves in their opening exchange as men who had
dedicated themselves to public service. It was this, as Odysseus
said, that made a man really a man. In the original words of
Euripides, which happen to survive, "We honor those who strive
and accomplish something more, and we consider them men in
our city" (τιμῶμεν ἄνδρας τ' ἐν πόλει νομίζομεν). In the para-

39. Lucian, Pereg. 33.

phrase by Dio, "We all admire the illustrious people and those who dare to grasp at more, and we consider them truly men" (τῷ ὄντι ἄνδρας ἡγούμεθα).⁴⁰ Philoctetes responds to this later by saying that he had suffered his terrible wound at the altar of Chryse while sacrificing in the common cause.⁴¹

The parallelism of the claims of Odysseus and Philoctetes is sharply underscored by Dio Chrysostom in his paraphrase. He makes Philoctetes use precisely the same phrase as Odysseus had used at the very beginning. Both men are made to say that they have acted on behalf of the common salvation and victory (ὑπὲρ τῆς κοινῆς σωτηρίας καὶ νίκης).⁴² Since Dio's paraphrase is exactly that and demonstrably not a literal or even a close reproduction of Euripides' own words, we may assume that this is not the phrasing of Euripides himself. Nor indeed is it likely to be, since this is an expression that is very much a part of the official ideological language of the Roman state. Dio must have chosen his periphrasis carefully. Many inscriptions of widely different dates and provenances with the Greek phrase ὑπὲρ σωτηρίας καὶ νίκης or the Latin equivalent *pro salute et victoria* establish the formal character of the phrase. Examples may be cited from Asia Minor, Syria, Egypt, and Algeria.⁴³ Normally the phrase is used to designate a dedication on behalf of the salvation and victory of an emperor or emperors. Here Dio varies the expression to make it apply to the Greeks or, by extension, mankind in general—ὑπὲρ τῆς κοινῆς σωτηρίας. It is, at one and the same time, an expression of Euripides' sentiment and a re-

40. See n. 19 above.
41. Dio Prus. *Orat.* 59.9.
42. *Ibid.* 59.1 (Odysseus), 9 (Philoctetes).
43. *OGIS* 614 (Der ͨa), 678 (Jebel Fatīra); *ILS* 2486 (Mena ͨa); *JRS* 63 (1973), 138 (Gerasa). Cf. C. B. Welles, *Royal Correspondence in the Hellenistic Period* (1934), p. 244, no. 59 (Pessinus).

flection of Roman imperial ideology. It demonstrates the immediate relevance of the Philoctetes story for the political life of the
Graeco-Roman world.

The story of Philoctetes in this era can be seen, therefore, as
illustrating the whole problem of sacrificing oneself for a greater
good. As Peregrinus said, every human being should become a
Philoctetes. He himself died to instruct mankind. Philoctetes had
suffered excruciating torment. Although he had formerly cried
out in terrible pain, the morality of the Graeco-Roman world
gradually silenced his cries and left only the image of suffering
courageously endured. All these great themes, articulated and
developed from the time of Nero and Dictys well into the third
century, ought now to guide us surely and unerringly to a better
understanding of the way in which the Greeks and Romans of
this period responded to an extraordinary story that came out of
Palestine in the middle of the first century.

A man of flesh and blood, who laid claim to divinity, sacrificed
himself, it was said, for the good of mankind. But Jesus, unlike
Peregrinus, cried out upon the cross where he met his terrible
death: *Eli, Eli lama sabachthani?*—"My God, my God, why have
you forsaken me?"[44] So direct and uncontrolled an expression of
grief was, as we have come to see, utterly at variance with the
standards of the Graeco-Roman society in which and by which
Jesus was crucified. We should now not be surprised to find that
it was this all-too-human response that sufficed to convince
Lucian's contemporary Celsus of the weakness and even effeminacy of Jesus Christ. Because of Celsus's observations in his
treatise the *True Discourse*, the third-century apologist Origen
was obliged to take up the whole question of Jesus's toleration

44. Mark 15.34, Matt. 27.46. Cf. Luke 23.46 (φωνήσας φωνῇ
μεγάλη).

of pain. If Jesus were in any sense divine, Celsus argued that whatever was done to him would have been neither painful nor grievous. He went on to ask, "Why does he utter loud laments and wailings, and why does he pray that he may avoid the fear of death, saying something like this: 'Oh Father, if this cup could pass by me'?"[45] As Origen was alert to point out, Celsus misquoted the original text from Matthew, nor did the Gospels ever say that Jesus explicitly "uttered wailings."[46] But that Jesus cried out, no one could deny.

Philoctetes provides a polytheistic mirror for the Christian passion. The weakness and implicit hypocrisy in Jesus's conduct, as it appeared to Celsus, became even more important in pagan polemic as Christianity gathered strength. Nowhere was it so sensationally represented as at the end of the satiric dialogue on the Caesars by the emperor Julian. There Jesus appears as completely wanton, inviting all murderers, rapists, and other sacrilegious persons to have their crimes washed away.[47] Curiously the weakness of the hero Philoctetes also reappears at almost the same time in the writings of the Christian Ausonius, who invokes him as a paradigm of solitary vice in one of those obscene poems of which his classical training had made him a master.[48]

If later polytheists took no pride in Philoctetes, they could be moved by his suffering—when he suffered in silence, as he did in painting and sculpture. In the Roman imperial period, the Stoic

---

45. Origen, *Contra Celsum* 2.24 (trans. H. Chadwick).
46. Ibid.
47. Julian, *Caes.* (*Symp.*) 38, 336 a–b. Curiously in eighteenth-century editions Jesus is replaced by a son of Constantine (as a result of the erroneous expansion of the manuscript ιυ): cf. Abbé de la Blèterie, *Histoire de Jovien,* vol. 1 (Paris, 1748), pp. 313 and 385–94.
48. Auson. *Epig.* 79, l. 3 (Prete): *Herculis heredi quam* [sc. *Venerem*] *Lemnia suasit egestas,* explained in l. 7 by *deglubit.*

doctrine of the endurance of pain, as expressed by Cicero, Marcus Aurelius, and others, had utterly transformed the howling and malodorous hero that Lessing admired in Sophocles' play. For the postclassical period, which was also the period of the Laocoön group, Winckelmann was surely right. The surviving epigrams on representations of Philoctetes in art (three in Greek, one in Latin) all stress the artist's depiction of pain, but none mentions any sign of crying out. The poets say that spectators can almost feel Philoctetes' pain, but never that they almost hear his cries. The epigrammatist Julianus wrote: "I know Philoctetes when I look on him, for he makes manifest his pain to all, even to those who gaze on him from a distance. He is all shaggy like a wild man; look at the locks of his head, squalid and hardcolored. His skin is parched and shrunken to look at, and perchance feels dry even to the finger's touch. Beneath his dry eyes the tears stand frozen, the sign of sleepless agony."[49]

Philoctetes' rage, his running sore, his wild hair, his skin, even frozen tears in his dry eyes, all receive admiring comment. But for the viewer Philoctetes clearly suffers in silence. It was in this way that he could be accepted as a savior. The Greeks and the Romans of the early centuries of the Christian era had made their savior in their own image and likeness.

49. *Anth. Pal.* 16.113.

CHAPTER FOUR

The Reality of Dreams

The reader of ancient fiction enters a world in which dreams appear significantly in the exposition of plot and character. The relevance of these episodes to life in the imperial age is hard to assess, because dreams are inherently mysterious and elusive. Dreams, both real and imagined, can often strain credulity, and yet they are bound to tell us something about the world that generates them. There can be no doubt of their importance even among the highly educated. The great doctor Galen in the second century of the Christian era wrote that, although some people paid no attention to dreams, he held them in high regard. "I know," he said, "that I have often made a diagnosis from dreams; and, guided by two very clear dreams, I once made an incision into the artery between the thumb and index finger of the right hand." Nor, it seems, was this a unique success: "I have saved many people," Galen goes on to say, "by applying a cure prescribed in a dream."[1]

Coming from one of the founders of scientific medicine and one of the most broadly cultured physicians that ever lived, these observations have a special importance. They prove that taking dreams seriously was hardly a characteristic of the ignorant or poor. Dreams had an immediate, practical relevance for daily

---

1. Galen 16.222 (Kühn).

life, even among the very highly educated. Galen does not tell us exactly how the successful cures were revealed to him in his dreams, or who, if anyone, prescribed them. His contemporary the great sophist Aelius Aristides often saw the god Asclepius in dreams in Pergamum, and it was from that divine source that he undertook many bizarre treatments for his illness over more than a decade.[2] Also in Pergamum Aristides' rival sophist Polemo set up a statue of Demosthenes, his great predecessor, together with an inscription to commemorate a dream that he had there.[3] The Stoic emperor Marcus Aurelius expressed gratitude in his *Meditations* for help furnished in dreams.[4] Galen's younger contemporaries the emperor Septimius Severus and the historian Cassius Dio were drawn to one another through their shared confidence in the importance of dreams. Dio tells us that he had narrated the dreams that foretold Severus's rise to power in a small work that antedated his own great history, which was itself set in motion by a dream.[5] It is reported that in his autobiography the emperor himself gave an account of the marvelous dreaming that anticipated his accession.[6]

Significant dreaming was nothing new in the second century. It went back in the classical tradition as far as Homer. It figured

---

2. See the *Sacred Tales* of Aristides, as well as G. Michenaud and J. Dierkens, *Les rêves dans les "Discours sacrés" d'Aelius Aristide, IIe siècle ap. J.-C.: Essai d'analyse psychologique* (1972).

3. C. Habicht, *Die Inschriften des Asklepieions, Altertümer von Pergamon* vol. 8.3, (1969), pp. 75–76 no. 33; cited by Phrynichus, *Eclog.* p. 494 (Rutherford).

4. Marcus Aurelius, *Ad Se Ipsum* 1.17.9; also 20 (τὸ δι' ὀνειράτων βοηθήματα). Cf. R. B. Rutherford, *The Meditations of Marcus Aurelius: A Study* (1989), pp. 195–200 ("Dreams and Sickness").

5. Cass. Dio 73.23.1.

6. *Ibid.* 73.23.1.

prominently in the historical narratives of Herodotus and the classical Greek theater. As Galen said, some disparaged it, but clearly most did not. From time immemorial dreams tended to uncover the anxieties or ambitions of the dreamer, as well as to provide advice for the future. Sometimes the appearance of a god imparted a divine authority to the dream, and sometimes a dream seemed actually to foretell the future. But generally predictions took the form of prescriptions. In other words the dreamer was told what to do, and the dream thus had its predictive force when the prescription was carried out. The predictive interpretation of dreams that were not in any way prescriptive was another matter altogether. This was a form of occultism, a pseudoscience like the reading of palms or the interpretation of animals' entrails. It involved seeing one thing—or rather hearing reports of seeing one thing—and determining, on the basis of it, some other thing that would happen in the future.

In the first book of his work on divination Cicero made this point unambiguously. He distinguished two forms of prophetic activity that human beings turn to *sine ratione et scientia*—"without reason or knowledge."[7] These are oracular utterances by a possessed intermediary and individual dreams. Cicero discussed both at length, and in his treatment of dreams (*somnia*) accorded ample attention to the inescapable fact that many dreams depict or predict what is simply false. *At multa falsa;*[8] yet, we are told, many are not so much false as obscure and have to be interpreted. Even so, some are really false. Clearly guidance is called for, and the ancient world was not lacking in people to provide it. Most of them, like Artemidorus of Daldis, would have

7. Cicero, *De Div.* 1.4.
8. *Ibid.* 1.60: "'At multa falsa.' immo obscura fortasse nobis, sed sint falsa quaedam: contra vera quid dicimus?"

blushed to admit that their work was accomplished, in Cicero's words, without reason or science. The predictive interpretation of dreams is best known to us in the extensive dream analysis provided in the 'Ονειροκριτικά by Artemidorus, who was yet another contemporary of Galen in the second century.[9] Sigmund Freud thought, by his own admission, that he had found in Artemidorus's book a worthy antecedent in the study of the interpretation of dreams.[10] To the extent that Artemidorus collected accounts of interesting dreams, Freud was right. But Freud, as we all know, was interested in dreams as a reflection of the unconscious and as a revelation of suppressed anxieties. Artemidorus, by contrast, had little interest in that aspect of dream interpretation. His own theory carefully segregated what he called ἐνύπνια, those dreams that are no more and no less than a reflection of the fears and desires of the dreamer while awake, from the ὄνειροι, which he distinguished as those dreams that either directly or allegorically indicate what the future will be for the dreamer. These latter dreams, the ὄνειροι, were the principal concern of Artemidorus, and it is obvious why they were. In an age long before the existence of the psychoanalyst's couch, a dream interpreter who did nothing but uncover the hidden complexes of the dreamer would not be likely to have

9. Artemidorus's work is most accessible in the edition of R. A. Pack (Leipzig, 1963). For an excellent modern discussion of the *Oneirocritica*, see S. R. F. Price, "The Future of Dreams: From Freud to Artemidorus," *Past and Present* 113 (1986), 3–37.

10. S. Freud, *The Interpretation of Dreams*, in the standard English edition of the complete works, ed. J. Strachey, vol. 4 (1958), pp. 3–4, and especially the long notes on pp. 98–99. See p. 98, n. 1: "Artemidorus of Daldis . . . has left us the most complete and painstaking study of dream-interpretation as practised in the Graeco-Roman world."

had many clients. What everybody wanted to know was what was going to happen in the future. Hence a canny interpreter of dreams would inevitably devote himself to the science of prediction. This means that Artemidorus is at least as different from Freud as a fortune teller is from a psychoanalyst.

Artemidorus intended to be just as scientific in his research and deductions as Freud. He compiled extensive records of dreams of all imaginable kinds (and, it must be said, many that are quite unimaginable), and to this end he traveled the known world attending public gatherings, fairs, festivals, and any thronged occasion where he could confer with dreamers or (one suspects) also imaginative poseurs.[11] For Artemidorus the social level of the dreamer and the social context within which the dreams were experienced mattered enormously.[12] One has the impression that Artemidorus was not only assiduous in his work, but something of a snob. A well-adjusted dreamer, who lived a good life, could never, according to Artemidorus, have such uninteresting dreams as ἐνύπνια because he would not be subject to the kinds of fears or anxieties that would be reflected in nonpredictive dreams of that sort. Such breathtaking naiveté must have astonished Freud, but it probably reflects the clientele that Artemidorus proposed

---

11. Artem. *Oneir.* 1 *prooem.* p. 2, ll. 11–27 (Pack).

12. Artem. *Oneir.* 4 *prooem.* p. 239, l. 14 – p. 240, l. 28 (Pack). Cf. Freud (n. 10 above), p. 98: "An interesting modification of the process of decoding, which to some extent corrects the purely mechanical character of its method of transposing, is to be found in the book written upon the interpretation of dreams [*Oneirocritica*] by Artemidorus of Daldis. This method takes into account not only the content of the dream but also the character and circumstances of the dreamer; so that the same dream-element will have a different meaning for a rich man, a married man, or, let us say, an orator, from what it has for a poor man, a bachelor, or a merchant."

to serve. The better sort of people had only ὄνειροι, or predictive dreams. Those were the only kinds of dreams he was interested in discussing.[13] From his lofty position Artemidorus was able to castigate his rivals as no better than tricksters and magicians. Gaining a good reputation as a dream interpreter was probably not all that easy. It required the aggressive salesmanship that Artemidorus obviously had in abundance. The reader of Petronius's *Satyricon* will recall Ascyltos's tart question about fancy speakers: "Would I have to listen to well-turned phrases that are like scraps of broken glass and the interpretation of dreams?"[14] He is talking about trash.

Artemidorus aspired not to write trash. He chose as his targets an essentially elite audience. These were people who never had dreams reflecting troublesome fears and desires, because, in his view, their superior style of life freed them from such emotions. It can hardly be possible, therefore, that Artemidorus is a reliable witness to the ordinary world of conventions and presuppositions in the second century. Yet enthusiasm for Artemidorus's book of dream analysis in recent years has paradoxically cast him in this remarkable role. One thoughtful writer, Jack Winkler in his *Constraints of Desire,* describes Artemidorus as "a dream analyst who spent years investigating the social meanings which average people saw in their dreams." He goes on to say, "His theory and practice of interpretation uniquely qualify him as a witness to common conceptions because he sees his role as one of letting the social meanings held by his clients speak for themselves."[15] The same writer asserts with confidence, "Artemidorus's categorization of sexual acts corresponds to widespread

13. Artem. *Oneir., loc. cit.* (n. 12 above).

14. Petron. *Satyr.* 10.1: "an videlicet audirem sententias, id est vitrea fracta et somniorum interpretamenta?"

15. J. Winkler, *The Constraints of Desire* (1990), p. 11.

and long-enduring social norms—that is, to the public percep-
tion of the meaning of sexual behavior."[16]

The architect of this representation of Artemidorus's work
would appear to be Michel Foucault, who declared, in his *History of Sexuality,* that the dream analyses of Artemidorus let us
"see certain generally accepted schemas of evaluation." He generalized this point immediately by saying, "One can affirm these
are very near to the general principles which already in the
classical period organized the moral experience of *aphrodisia.*
Artemidorus's book is therefore a landmark. It testifies to a
scheme of thinking that was long enduring and current in his
day."[17] Foucault stated explicitly that the type of dreamer to
whom Artemidorus addressed himself was an ordinary person—*un individu ordinaire,* concerned with health, life, death,
and material prosperity. His clientele was middle-level (*moy-
enne*). He is alleged to discuss the preoccupations of ordinary
people (*des gens ordinaires*).[18]

A reader of Artemidorus may well wonder how what appears
there can conceivably represent "generally accepted schemas of
evaluation" or constitute "a scheme of thinking that was long
enduring and current in his day." We look in vain for any basis
for such an assessment of Artemidorus's work. Nowhere else in
the whole of classical antiquity can one find, for example, a man
who "dreamed that he was feeding bread and cheese to his penis
as if it were an animal,"[19] nor is there anything to compare with
Artemidorus's detailed account of dreams of sexual intercourse

16. *Ibid.* 24.
17. M. Foucault, *Le souci de soi, Histoire de la sexualité,* vol. 3
(1984), p. 1. These opinions are quoted in English by Winkler (n. 15
above), p. 43.
18. Foucault (n. 17 above), pp. 19–20.
19. Artem. *Oneir.* 5.62, p. 315, ll. 17–20 (Pack).

with one's mother. Incest, to be sure, played an important role in Greek culture and Greek tragedy before it was taken over as a particular preserve by Freud. But Artemidorus's approach to sex with one's mother is something altogether unexampled. His treatment of this unappetizing subject is central to Winkler's argument and is reprinted in full as an appendix to his book.[20] (This part of Artemidorus's work, incidentally, was omitted from Krauss's nineteenth-century German translation, which Freud used.)

In his clinical way Artemidorus states, "The analysis of the mother is intricate, elaborate, and susceptible of many discriminations. It has eluded many dream analysts. It goes as follows— intercourse in itself is not sufficient to show the intended significance of the dream, but the postures and positions of the bodies, being different, make the outcome different." From this point Artemidorus goes on to discuss in remarkable detail the various positions that a son might take in having intercourse with his mother.

Frontal penetration, which Artemidorus declares some people consider perfectly natural, will predict a falling out with one's father, if he is still alive (because, we are hardly surprised to learn, of the jealousy involved). If the father is ill, the dream predicts that he will then die. On the other hand, a frontal approach constitutes a good dream for all craftsmen and laborers, "for it is usual to refer to one's craft as 'mother,' and what else could sexual intimacy with one's craft signify except having no leisure and being productive from it." Artemidorus then moves on to less natural forms of congress with one's mother. Anal penetration, he says, is very bad for the future; and, if the mother is on top and riding the son, this is very difficult to interpret. Sick men

20. *Ibid.* 1.79, p. 91, l.3 – p. 95, l. 13 (Pack).

who have this dream always die, but healthy ones live out the remainder of their lives in great ease and just as they choose.

These are only a few of the possible forms of incestuous congress that interest Artemidorus, but there is absolutely nothing in the literature and art of classical antiquity to suggest that what we find here represents, in Foucault's words, "a scheme of thinking that was long enduring and current in [Artemidorus's] day." It is more than likely that the dreams reported by Artemidorus were really dreamed by someone. Psychoanalysts with whom I have spoken can see here, as Freud did in the case of other Artemidorean dreams, the signs of authentic dream experiences. But like the dreams recorded and analyzed by Freud himself, these experiences by their very nature as dreams lie outside the conventions and protocols of ordinary life. If we were to describe current thinking at the end of the nineteenth century on the basis of the dreams in Freud's *Interpretation of Dreams,* we should certainly produce an unrecognizable and unhistorical world.

In short, there is every reason to believe that Artemidorus's book is exceptional precisely because it includes so many dreams that would have otherwise been known only to the dreamer. Those dreams may take their origin in the substrate of common conventions and protocols that some have sought to find there, but they hardly provide a simple index of the patterns of waking life. Even granting, as we should, that the dreams of Foucault's ordinary people can be extraordinary—that dream fantasies can indeed often astonish the dreamer after waking up (as well as others who may hear of them)—we can find nothing in the manual that Artemidorus put together that allows the sexual acts he describes there to be said to correspond "with widespread and long-enduring social norms." Parallels are utterly lacking, and without them the wish-fulfilling fantasies of scholars can have little probative value. The attempt to enlist Artemidorus as a hitherto-unnoticed sexual libertarian and to deduce from his work that the whole Graeco-Roman world took everything he talked about as perfectly consonant with daily life is one of the most serious, if well-intentioned, misrepresentations of antiquity that the modern world has yet beheld.

Since dreams are so important in the fictional literature of Artemidorus's own day, most conspicuously in the novels, it would be worth looking at a selection of the dreams that appear in those works to see whether or not they provide any support for understanding the dream book of Artemidorus as a precious repository of common views. One of this century's leading interpreters of the ancient novel, Bryan Reardon, has recently written quite correctly, "Dreams and their interpretation much interested antiquity, certainly late antiquity, and are a standard feature of novels."[21] That is certainly correct. But do their dreams parallel the researches of Artemidorus? Dreams in fiction, as well as those that eminent public figures like Marcus Aurelius may feel comfortable in telling to the whole world, are the product of the mind when it is fully awake. These are the dreams that ought to tell us something about current thought and morality, as well as attitudes toward dreaming itself. Can they possibly look like what we read in Artemidorus?

In a recent paper on this very question one scholar was moved to answer in the affirmative. She summarized her conclusions as follows: "Dreams in the novels relate to personal goals, anxieties, or fears. These oneiric aspirations reflect the contemporary waking world where the predominant feeling is for 'self.' The same observation can be made in the *Oneirocritica* of Artemidorus, the novels' approximate contemporary. In addition, the novelists' treatment of and attitude toward ways of identifying and inter-

21. B. P. Reardon, *Collected Ancient Greek Novels* (1989), p. 34, n. 27.

preting dreams also conforms to Artemidorus's system. The novels contain examples from all the diverse dream categories that he envisaged."[22] Apart from the writer's observation about personal goals, anxieties, and fears in the novels, virtually everything here is wrong. Artemidorus's Ὀνειροκριτικά are not principally concerned with personal goals, anxieties, and fears. The way in which the novelists identify and interpret dreams does not conform to Artemidorus's system. And, after what we have already looked at, it must be obvious that it is absurd to suggest that the novels contain examples from *all* the diverse dream categories that Artemidorus envisaged.

What follows now is a sample of dreams from the major novelists in Greek, who ought to provide the best points of comparison with Artemidorus's Greek constituency. In what is probably the earliest of the novels, Chariton's *Chaereas and Callirhoe,* the pirate Theron, who has abducted the heroine from her tomb (where she had unfortunately been placed when unconscious), contemplates throwing her into the sea at the break of day because she would be a difficult cargo. But he falls asleep and has a dream in which he sees a closed door. This he believes to be an admonition to wait for at least a day.[23] So he does wait for a day, and the story is able to continue in its meandering way without the sacrifice of the heroine at an early stage. In a later dream the heroine, Callirhoe, herself sees her lover, Chaereas, in chains.[24] The dream is clairvoyant, because Chaereas actually is in chains, but Callirhoe misinterprets it. She says explicitly that this must signify death, yet clearly it does not, because the story

22. S. MacAlistair, "Oneirocriticism and the Ancient Greek Novel," a one-page précis in *The Ancient Novel, Classical Paradigms and Modern Perspectives,* ed. J. Tatum and G. M. Vernazza (1990), p. 68.
23. Chariton, *Chaer. and Call.* 1.12.5.
24. *Ibid.* 3.7.4–5.

goes on. Callirhoe's interpretation is simply a reflection of her anxiety, just as her dream had itself been a reflection of her love for Chaereas. Still farther along in the same novel Callirhoe dreams that she is in Syracuse, her homeland, entering the shrine of Aphrodite.[25] There she beholds her beloved Chaereas. Unfortunately she wakes up just before she embraces him. This is obviously another reflection of her love for Chaereas and her desire to be united with him.

From the romance of Xenophon of Ephesus we may excerpt the dream of Anthia, the heroine, in which a beautiful woman draws away her beloved, Habrocomes.[26] This is transparently a sign of her anxiety that some other woman will win the affections of her true love. In Achilles Tatius, near the beginning of the novel, the hero, Cleitophon, has a dream of his beloved,[27] in much the same way as Callirhoe dreams several times in Chariton of her beloved. In the second book of Achilles Tatius's romance Pantheia has a grisly dream in which her daughter is sliced in two by a bandit.[28] This may perhaps anticipate, in an artistic way, the false sacrifice of her daughter at the hands of the Boukoloi a book later; but, since the daughter survives, the dream could hardly be called predictive. It is, rather, another dream of anxiety and fear. In the fourth book of the same romance the heroine, Leucippe, dreams that she is going to be butchered, but the goddess Artemis appears.[29] The dream reflects the dangers and anxieties of Leucippe. She is, after all, a lady who seems to die repeatedly in Achilles Tatius's romance, although she never really does. Her beloved, Cleitophon, had had a dream rather like that of the

25. *Ibid.* 5.5.5–6.
26. Xen. Eph. *Ephes.* 5.8.
27. Achill. Tat. *Leuc. and Cleit.* 1.6.5.
28. *Ibid.* 2.23.4–5.
29. *Ibid.* 4.1.4.

pirate Theron in Chariton, in which he sees closed doors at a temple of Aphrodite, and he construes this as an admonition to him to wait before proceeding.[30]

This sampling of dreams from three Greek novels, of roughly the same century as the work of Artemidorus, points unmistakably to a lack of interest in predicting the future from dreams. Like Freud, the Greek novelists are far more concerned with reflections of the fears and desires of the dreamers, particularly fears of death and desires for the lover's embrace. The only dreams that are not of this form are admonitions, in which the dreamer infers what he should do on the basis of what he has seen in a dream. We have noted in two cases a closed door interpreted as an admonition to wait. None of these dreams can be paralleled by anything in Artemidorus.

But perhaps we should not expect to find parallels there. Artemidorus is, after all, interested only in ὄνειροι, not in ἐνύπνια. Nonetheless it is worth noting that the chains that Callirhoe believed to be a sign of death are indeed registered in Artemidorus, but as nothing more sinister than a sign of obstruction to one's activities. A chain can also make reference to a spouse, declares Artemidorus on suspect etymological grounds, but again there is no suggestion of death.[31] As for the kind of bodily mutilation that threatened Leucippe in the novel by Achilles Tatius, Artemidorus has much to say, with his interpretations varying according to the part of the body that is mutilated. Yet, with all his detail, his observations on injuries to the midsection bear very little resemblance to Leucippe's plight. If you dream of being cut open when you are poor or childless, you may expect to acquire chil-

30. *Ibid.* 4.1.6–7.
31. Artem. *Oneir.* 3.35, p. 219, ll.1–5 (Pack) [ἄλυσις]. Cf. 4.5, p. 248, l. 23 (Pack).

dren and property. But, if you are rich, shame or deprivation will be in store. It is very bad for anyone to have his or her entrails seen by another.³² Pantheia would hardly have had any solace if she had been aware of such interpretations when she dreamed that her daughter was cut in two.

Admonitions interest Artemidorus scarcely at all, and yet they are very important for the novelists. Sometimes a sign conveys the advice, as in the case of the closed door, or more often a god appears in a dream, as so often happened to Aelius Aristides, to communicate the advice directly. This happens, for example, in the novel by Achilles Tatius when the goddess Artemis appears in a dream to Leucippe's father, Sostratus, to reveal that he should go to find his daughter in Ephesus and his brother's son as well.³³ In the latest of the romances, Heliodorus's novel about Ethiopia, Calasiris records that Apollo and Artemis appeared together to him in a dream and entrusted both Theagenes and Charicleia, the lovers, to his care. Apollo made the commitment of Theagenes and Artemis of Charicleia. They addressed Calasiris by name in the dream and gave him an explicit injunction: "It is time now for you to return to the land of your birth, for thus the ordinance of destiny demands. Go then, and take those whom we deliver to you; make them the companions of your journey; consider them as your own children."³⁴ Dreams of this kind are essentially like those in Aristides and probably also those in Galen, in which admonition, with the direct or perhaps indirect intercession of a divinity, is the principal ingredient and purpose of the dream. Although Artemidorus devotes consider-

---

32. *Ibid.* on the various parts of the body, 1.16–49, p.25, l.15 – p. 55, l. 4 (Pack). Cf. 1.44, p. 50, l. 10 – p. 51, l. 12 (Pack), on dreaming of being cut up.

33. Achill. Tat. *Leuc. and Cleit.* 7.12.4, 14.5–6.

34. Heliod. *Aeth.* 3.11.5.

able attention to the appearance of deities in dreams,[35] he has no interest at all in the advice that they may give. His concern is entirely with the symbolic value of the deities for making predictions of the future.

Heliodorus's account of dreams is generally far more subtle and sophisticated than what we find in the other novelists. He exploits with consummate artistry the tendency of people to misinterpret their dreams, and in doing so he allows the reader as well as the characters to be misled. Shadi Bartsch, in her study of description (*ekphrasis*) in Achilles Tatius and Heliodorus, has lucidly analyzed the ambivalence of dream interpretation.[36] At the end of Book 2 Heliodorus makes Calasiris compare dreams with oracles as revelations that can only be interpreted properly once the outcome is known. Skepticism of this kind had already turned up early in the work when the robber Thyamis forced the interpretation of a dream he had about Charicleia and Isis "to conform," as Heliodorus says, "with his own desires." Later on he is obliged to reinterpret the same dream all over again.[37]

The uncertainty of dream interpretation predominates even in a scene in which one of the characters hits upon a solution that reflects rather more experience in the art. Charicleia dreamed that an evil man cut out her right eye with a sword. She promptly but erroneously interpreted this to mean that her beloved Theagenes would be killed—"my eye, my soul, my all." Not so,

35. See the long treatment of gods in Artem. *Oneir.* 2.33–44, pp. 155–79 (Pack).

36. S. Bartsch, *Decoding the Ancient Novel* (1989), chap. 3 ("Dreams, Oracles, and Oracular Dreams: Misinterpretation and Motivation"), pp. 80–108.

37. Heliod. *Aeth.* 2.36.2 (Calasiris: χρησμοὶ γὰρ καὶ ὄνειροι τὰ πολλὰ τοῖς τέλεσι κρίνονται). Cf. 1.18.5 (first interpretation of Thyamis), 1.30.4 (reinterpretation).

says Cnemon, awakened from a sleep of his own. The loss of the right eye means the loss of her father.[38] As Bartsch and J. R. Morgan have both independently observed, this interpretation actually coincides with the professional judgment of Artemidorus on such a dream,[39] and in a sense it even turns out to have a specious element of truth in it—if one accepts Calasiris as a kind of father to Charicleia, although he, in fact, is not her father. But even Cnemon brushes aside his own interpretation by saying, "Here we are analyzing dreams and figments of the imagination and not pausing for a moment to think how to solve our own problems."[40] He, who obviously knows something of the trade, dismisses it as unproductive.

As Charicleia's dream shows, prophetic dreams are not altogether absent from the novels, nor should any reader of Cicero's *De Divinatione* expect them to be. But they are relatively infrequent. Perhaps the most startling occurs near the opening of Achilles Tatius's story of Leucippe and Cleitophon, when the narrator, Cleitophon himself, records a dream of Artemidorean strangeness, in which his half-sister's body and his own are seen to have grown together from the navel down. (Details are not provided.) A terrible woman with bloodshot eyes and snakes for hair hacks the two bodies apart where they were joined at the groin. This dream is introduced as prophetic: "Often the celestial powers delight to whisper to us at night about what the future holds—not that we may contrive a defense to forestall it (for no one can rise above fate), but that we may bear it more lightly

---

38. *Ibid.* 2.16.3–4.
39. Artem. *Oneir.* 1.26, p. 34, ll. 7–9. Cf. Bartsch (n. 36 above), pp. 99–100, n. 8; and J. R. Morgan in B. P. Reardon, ed., *Collected Ancient Greek Novels*, p. 389 n. 40.
40. Heliod. *Aeth.* 2.16.7.

when it comes."⁴¹ The dreadful dream portended that Cleitophon would not be marrying his half-sister, as his father had
wished.

Later in the same novel one of the characters, Sostratus, complains to Artemis that what he had taken to be a prediction in
a dream actually was not. The passage is less interesting for its
allusion to dreams of the predictive kind than for the Greek word
used there for dreams. It violates completely the definition laid
down by Artemidorus. The allegedly predictive dream is called
ἐνύπνιον. In upbraiding Artemis Sostratus can even speak of τῶν
ἐνυπνίων τὰ μαντεύματα ("the prophecies of ἐνύπνια"). And
that he sees no difference whatever between an ἐνύπνιος and an
ὄνειρος is conclusively shown in his very next utterance, in which
he says to the goddess, "I trusted your dreams." This time the
word is ὀνείροις.⁴²

It is fair to say that the fiction of the Roman imperial period
reinforces completely the impression that nonfictional texts, such
as those of Aristides, Cassius Dio, and Galen, provide in the
matter of taking dreams seriously. That is to say, they were indeed
taken seriously, but principally as reflections of the fears or desires
of the dreamer or else as sources of instruction or advice for future
conduct. In other words, these texts illustrate the same kinds of
dreams as interested Freud. They do not represent a view of
dreams chiefly as predictive materials. Artemidorus's position is
that of a professional dream interpreter, a kind of superior fortune
teller, a man who aspires to an affluent clientele that, in his view,
does not have anything to do with anxiety and wish fulfillment.
Artemidorus is a snob. It is no surprise that of the people he
mentions by name several are famous characters of the time—the

41. Achill. Tat. *Leuc. and Cleit.* 1.3.2–4.
42. *Ibid.* 7.14.5.

philosopher Plutarch of Chaeronea, the orator and teacher of emperors Cornelius Fronto from North Africa, and the affluent Ruso of Laodicea.[43] The person called Cassius Maximus to whom Artemidorus dedicated the first three books of his Ὀνειροκριτικά was evidently someone of consequence too, and quite probably none other than the great rhetorician Maximus of Tyre.[44]

The highly exceptional character of Artemidorus's work shows up in another of his dogmatic pronouncements. For centuries the Greeks and the Romans believed that dreams and visions that occurred after midnight were true, whereas those that came to the sleeper before midnight were false. The literature on this popular belief is substantial, and most readers of Virgil will be reminded of the gates of true and false dreams in the sixth book of the *Aeneid*.[45] Artemidorus is perfectly well aware that

43. Artem. *Oneir*. 4.72, p. 293, l. 21 (Pack), mentioning Plutarch; 4.22, p. 257, l. 13 (Pack), Φρόντων ὁ ἀρθριτικός, clearly the valetudinarian orator and teacher of Marcus Aurelius; 4.1, p. 241, ll. 25–26 (Pack), Ῥούσων ὁ Λαοδικεύς, on whom, with reference to this passage, see L. Robert, *Laodicée du Lycos: Le nymphée*, Université Laval, Fouilles (1969), pp. 311–12. It is unfortunate that Pack's text prints Δρούσων in Artemidorus. Even Robert's earlier citation of the correct reading in his *Noms indigènes de l'Asie Mineure gréco-romaine* (1963), pp. 41–42 appeared too late for Pack, whose edition was also published in 1963.

44. *PIR*² C 509. Observe that Artemidorus clearly implies that his patron was a Phoenician (*Oneir*. 2.70, p. 203, ll. 13–15 [Pack]), at the conclusion of Book 2, where Cassius Maximus (ἀνδρῶν σοφώτατε) is again addressed explicitly: καὶ γὰρ εἶναί τινα Λυδοῖς προξενίαν πρὸς Φοίνικας οἱ τὰ πάτρια ἡμῖν ἐξηγούμενοί φασιν. Artemidorus himself was a Lydian (from Daldis).

45. See the full documentation on this point in Pack's note on p. 16 of his edition of Artemidorus. Among his references is, naturally, Virg. *Aen*. 6.898.

this was the received opinion, but he, presenting himself as a truly scientific interpreter of dreams, takes a different view—a view that could hardly be more out of line with contemporary sentiment. It makes no difference when the dreams occur, according to Artemidorus, whether at night or even in the daytime; nor does it matter whether they occur in the twilight of the evening or the twilight of the dawn. The only thing that Artemidorus worries about is whether or not the sleeper has had a sufficiently light meal before dreaming. He is adamant that overindulgence at the dinner table eliminates the possibility of having true dreams, even when the dreams occur the next morning at dawn.[46]

That such pseudoscientific precision is utterly at variance with contemporary opinion can be seen arrestingly in the tract of the polytheist Celsus against the Christians. It will be recalled that he found so much implausibility in the Gospels that he saw in the tale of Jesus a fiction that looked very little different from the novelists we have been examining earlier. The epiphany of Jesus after his death seemed to Celsus nothing more than a routine dream or hallucination. Celsus attributed the whole story of the risen Jesus essentially to a report of a hysterical female, Mary Magdalene. The appearance of a presumably dead man was, for Celsus, no more than a dream "in a certain state of mind or through wishful thinking . . . due to some mistaken notion—an experience that has happened to thousands."[47] Visions of the dead in dreams, if not exactly an ordinary occurrence, certainly are mentioned frequently enough in the literature of antiquity to give some plausibility to Celsus's hostile interpretation.

In making his rebuttal, the Christian apologist Origen accused Celsus of suggesting that certain people were actually

46. Artem. *Oneir.* 1.7, p. 16, l. 10 – p. 17, l. 2 (Pack).
47. Origen, *Contra Celsum* 2.55.

dreaming in the daytime, something he implies neither of them would have thought at all plausible. Although Celsus was a younger contemporary of Artemidorus, he was unlikely to have had the advantage of reading his *Oneirocritica*. And, if he had, Origen could still attack him by referring to the conventional opinion. Origen admitted that Celsus's opinion "would not be unreasonable if the visions had occurred by night; but his idea of a vision in the daytime is not convincing, when the people were in no way mentally unbalanced and were not suffering from delirium or melancholy."[48] Needless to say, Origen was not prepared to acknowledge that Mary Magdalene was "a hysterical female."

From a non-Christian perspective, visions of the dead in sleep were far easier to credit than resurrection in the flesh. In the generation after Celsus's interpretation of the life of Jesus, the sophist Philostratus composed a life of the pagan sage and wise man Apollonius of Tyana. Apollonius was reported to have wrought miracles so remarkably similar to those of Jesus Christ that, in the days of the Tetrarchs in the early fourth century, another polytheist writer was able to take up the cause of Celsus by advancing Apollonius as the Antichrist.[49] Nonetheless, when Apollonius finally died, toward the end of the first century of the Christian era, he may perhaps have left the tomb in which he was placed. Philostratus, at any rate, allows for this possibility.[50] Yet no one dared to report that he saw Apollonius resurrected in the flesh. But a little after nine months had passed, a boy fell

48. *Ibid.* 2.60 (trans. H. Chadwick).

49. Hierocles (*PLRE* Hierocles 4), whose views were countered by Eusebius in his *Contra Hieroclem*. For a full discussion, see T. D. Barnes, *Constantine and Eusebius* (1981), pp. 164–67.

50. Philost. *Vit. Apoll.* 8.30, with 31 *ad fin.*

asleep while engaged in a discussion of wisdom with his friends. In the midst of his sleep Apollonius came to him and declaimed in his dream on the nature of the soul.[51] If we are not told whether this took place in the daytime or at night, it is undoubtedly because the discussion took place at night. The boy's companions were drawing geometrical figures in the sand, but this detail neither tells us whether the group was indoors or outside, nor does it tell the hour. Dreaming in the daytime would have been as implausible for Philostratus as for Origen.

Dreaming was undoubtedly an important part of the spiritual and intellectual life of Greeks and Romans in the time of the Roman empire. It was as important to the highly educated as to the illiterate. But a professional dream interpreter should no more condition our understanding of this important aspect of Graeco-Roman society than a soothsayer should instruct us on the ancient view of birds or animals. Artemidorus was a diligent researcher and, without any doubt, exceptionally thorough in compiling the most varied and outlandish assortment of dreams ever examined by a single person. Certainly Freud cannot compete with Artemidorus in the promulgation of remarkable dreams. Just as art dealers are very rarely disinterested, though often exceptionally learned and intelligent, so too was Artemidorus never disinterested: he had a product to sell, and he was proud of his product. It was the predictive interpretation of dreams. Prediction was something that was of far more importance to the upper strata of society than the lower. Those who possessed property or power had more to lose—or gain. It was the rich, the ruling class, the emperors who had the most at stake in ascertaining what the future held, and who could afford to

---

51. *Ibid.* 8.31.

summon to their aid the professional astrologers and soothsayers, and the likes of Artemidorus.

The Graeco-Roman world had just as much interest in the
projection of fears and desires in dreams as we would expect any
human society to have. They had, perhaps fortunately, no Freud
to interpret their dreams of this kind, but they did have their gods
to give explicit instructions when dreams could be ambiguous.
It would be wrong to assume that the obsession with the purely
predictive interpretation of dreams, as we find it in Artemidorus,
represents anything commonplace or fundamental at all in the
ancient world. It is a grossly illegitimate move to appropriate
Artemidorus as a representative of the masses of Greeks and
Romans and to impute to them protocols of sexuality or morality
on the basis of his dream book. Artemidorus does indeed deserve
a place in the history of the period, but his place remains as a
scholar of the occult, a chronicler of the unconscious mind, and
a professional profiteer in the business of making forecasts. He
is an archaeologist of sleep, whose research may remind us of
Freud but whose objectives clearly do not. He belongs in the
company of the best astrologers and soothsayers. For the historian, it is paradoxically the fiction of the age that eloquently
confirms the outlook of the many historical figures who spoke for
it, like Galen, Marcus Aurelius, Cassius Dio, and Origen. It is the
fiction that delivers dreams of real historical significance in antiquity, for these were dreams that were created by a wakeful
author in conscious submission to the moral and emotional
expectations of his age.

CHAPTER FIVE

Resurrection

Among the most conspicuous features of the fiction of the Roman empire, not only the prose romances but the mythological confections as well, is resurrection after death in the original body. Much of the time the resurrection is explained by theatrical and often bloody deaths that turn out not to have been deaths at all. The *Scheintod,* as the Germans call it, the "apparent death," allows for all the excitement and tragedy of extinction and resurrection without unduly straining the credulity of the reader. The German scholar Erwin Rohde, whose interpretations of the Greek novel must even now command respect, identified the earliest appearance of apparent death and resurrection in the novel *The Wonders beyond Thule* by Antonius Diogenes. Rohde was perhaps the first to see that, after the work of Diogenes, *Scheintod* and resurrection became among the most beloved of themes in the Greek romances.[1] Since the fiction of Antonius Diogenes seems clearly to belong to that initial burst of creativity that we can trace from the reign of the emperor Nero

1. E. Rohde, *Der griechische Roman und seine Vorlaüfer,* 3d ed. (1914) p. 287, with n. 1: "Hier also das älteste Beispiel jener bei den Romanschreibern so beliebten Erfindung des Begräbnisses von Schein-toten." For more recent discussion of this theme, see F. Wehrli, "Einheit und Vorgeschichte der griechisch-römischen Romanliteratur," *MH* 22 (1965), 133–54, esp. 142–48.

down to the end of the first century of our era, the appearance of this motif concurrently with the development of the genre itself is not likely to be without significance.

Although we know the complicated plot of *The Wonders beyond Thule* only from the exceedingly dense summary of it by the patriarch Photius, some memorable episodes can be disengaged. At a relatively early stage in the narrative an aristocratic woman of Phoenician Tyre, Dercyllis by name, turns up among the remote people known as Cimmerians. There a former slave of Dercyllis, a woman called Myrto, who had died long before, is introduced to instruct her former mistress on the nature of the Underworld. Myrto is not exactly brought back to life, since her activity with Dercyllis seems to have been confined to Hades. But subsequently Dercyllis takes a trip with some persons she had met in Hades, and they, the living and the dead, visit the nation of the Getae on the northern extremities of the Mediterranean world. Among the Getae Astraeus, who had come from Hades, meets his old friend Zamolxis, who is honored there as a god of his people.[2] Readers of Antonius Diogenes' work will have known from Herodotus that Zamolxis had died some five or six centuries earlier, only to be resurrected and become, as a result of this miracle, regarded as a divinity.[3] Once resurrected, he seems no longer to have been subjected to the ravages of time and could sustain his ancient friendship with so modern a traveler as Astraeus, who had, of course, himself made his way from the dead. A little later Dercyllis is subjected to an embarrassing

2. Photius, *Biblioth.* 109a–b [166], p. 141, ll. 41–42 (Henry), on Myrto. For Zamolxis, see 110a [166], pp. 143–44, ll. 22–37 (Henry).
    3. Herod. 4.94–96. The correct form of the name should perhaps be Zalmoxis: cf. I. I. Russu, *RE* 9.A.2, cols. 2301–2.

affliction, causing her to be dead during the daytime but restored to life in the night.⁴ At least one lover killed himself during the day over what he supposed was her corpse.

The appearance of the resurrected Zamolxis in the story by Antonius Diogenes underscores the Herodotean precedent for tall or miraculous tales, just as Dercyllis's visit to Hades and the return of Astraeus from the Underworld patently call to mind those visits to Hades that take their origins from the famous narrative in Homer's *Odyssey*. In fact, a return from the land of the dead was an important feature of several classical legends: Orpheus brought back Eurydice, and Heracles brought back Theseus. Equally, Euripides' play *Alcestis* has impressed upon every cultivated reader of Greek literature from antiquity to the present the tragic potential of one person's selflessness in being willing to die for another. In our own time the subject was no less movingly put on stage by Poulenc in his opera *The Dialogues of the Carmelites,* in which an older nun dies the death of a younger one. But all these negotiations for passage in and out of the world of the dead are obviously of a very different character from bodily resurrection after the corpse has grown cold. Not even the legendary philosopher Pythagoras, who was often associated with stories of returning from the dead, is remotely comparable to the Zamolxis of Herodotus and of Antonius Diogenes. Pythagoras believed in, and was said to have exemplified, a doctrine of reincarnation, which must certainly not be confused with resurrection.

Nor is resurrection the same as necromancy, by which the dead are magically summoned for a brief appearance in order to provide a prophecy of some kind. Necromancy as a form of

---

4. Photius, *Biblioth.* 110b [166], p. 144, ll. 1–10 (Henry).

ancient magic was hardly confined to the Greeks, as any reader of the Bible will know from the story of the witch of Endor.[5] Readers of the Greek novel will long remember the hair-raising episode in Heliodorus's *Aethiopica* in which an old woman causes the corpse of her son to stand bolt upright and to speak.[6] The consultation of deceased spirits has a long and lurid history in classical antiquity, but once again it is palpably not the same thing as resurrection in the flesh. For that there are virtually no examples before the second half of the first century of the present era.

The author of the article *Auferstehung* in the *Reallexikon für Antike und Christentum* states categorically that the whole concept of resurrection, although attested among other peoples, was altogether alien to Graeco-Roman thought.[7] He cites many examples from classical literature in support of this fundamentally accurate generalization. Aeschylus, in the *Eumenides*, summed it all up when he gave to Apollo the lines, "Once a man has died and the dust sucked up his blood, there is no resurrection [οὔτις ἔστ᾿ ἀνάστασις]."[8] Gods might die and be reborn, but not mortals of flesh and blood. The mortal dead might be conjured up in feverish dreams or imagined as ghostly apparitions, but they did not come back as before. When Cicero told the story of the Indian Brahman Calanus, who, before going to his funeral pyre, told Alexander the Great that he would be seeing him soon, neither Cicero nor, apparently, anyone else

---

5. I Kings (I Sam.) 28.7–14.

6. Heliod. *Aeth.* 6.14–15.

7. *RAC* s.v. "Auferstehung II (des Menschen)" col. 931: "Die A., manchen alten Völkern bekannt, liegt griech.-röm. Denken im ganzen fern" (A. Oepke).

8. Aesch. *Eum.* 647–48.

believed this to be a promise of immediate resurrection.⁹ The meaning of Calanus's enigmatic utterance only became clear, as Cicero says, when Alexander died in Babylon. The two met each other in death.

A similar inability to credit the fact of resurrection characterized those philosophers at Athens—Epicureans and Stoics—whom the apostle Paul is reported to have met there. According to the narrative in Acts, which must certainly reflect attitudes of the time, "Some philosophers said, 'What would this intellectual lightweight [σπερμολόγος] want to say?' And others said, 'He seems to be proclaiming foreign gods'—because he was preaching Jesus and resurrection [ἀνάστασις]."¹⁰ The philosophers appear to have imagined that Paul was importing two divinities, one Jesus Christ and the other a goddess Ἀνάστασις. So difficult was it for them to comprehend the message that Paul was really bringing to them. But obviously the news of resurrection had begun to spread.

Paul went to Athens just a few years before the accession of Nero. From that time onward the Greeks and the Romans acquired a lively interest in ἀνάστασις or, as pagan writers sometimes said, ἀναβίωσις ("return to life"). Rohde was absolutely correct when he observed that the subject of resurrection, with its attendant rationalizing explanation of apparent death, makes its earliest appearance in ancient fiction in Antonius Diogenes. And Diogenes drew on the one clear and distinctive example from classical literature, the deity of the Getae called Zamolxis. Just how much of Zamolxis's past Antonius Diogenes recounted to his readers we can never know, but he either repeated what Herodotus said or expected his readers to know it.

---

9. Cicero, *De Div.* 1.47 (*propediem te videbo*).
10. Acts 17.18.

Zamolxis's teachings, according to the Father of History, included the doctrine that none of his disciples or their posterity would ever perish, but that they would all go to a place where they would live forever in the bosom of their master.[11] In order to demonstrate the truth of his doctrine Zamolxis constructed a secret underground residence to which he retired when it seemed an appropriate moment for him to die—or rather appear to die. He lived in his underground chamber for some three years, after which he reappeared and was believed to have been resurrected. Herodotus takes a characteristically agnostic position about the story, but it is clear that the three-year residence underground is intended as a rationalist explanation for an otherwise miraculous event.[12] The death of Zamolxis, believed by his followers to be real, is, it is suggested, perhaps nothing but a *Scheintod*. On the other hand, there can be no question of a *Scheintod* for Diogenes if the resurrected Zamolxis is still around to converse with his friend Astraeus many centuries later.

After Antonius Diogenes the resurrection stories become ever more elaborate and lurid. Every reader of the romance of Chariton will remember the important episode in the third book in which the heroine's beloved Chaereas turns up at the tomb where she was believed to lie in death after an act of violence committed by Chaereas himself in a jealous rage. When Chaereas goes to the tomb, to offer wreaths and libations and (in accordance with his secret intention) to commit suicide on the spot, he finds the stones moved and the entrance laid open.[13] His beloved Callirhoe is no longer in the tomb. As the reader knows perfectly well, Callirhoe is still alive. For Chaereas the disappearance of the dead woman

11. Herod. 4.94.
12. *Ibid.* 4.95–96.
13. Chariton, *Chaer. and Call.* 3.3.1: παραγενόμενος δὲ εὗρε τοὺς λίθους κεκινημένους καὶ φανερὰν τὴν εἴσοδον.

cannot possibly be explained as the work of tomb robbers, even though one of his fellow citizens reasonably proposes this explanation. He jumps to the conclusion that she has been carried off by a god, as Dionysus took Ariadne or Zeus Semele. He abandons his idea of committing suicide. In an apostrophe to the absent Callirhoe, he cries out, "You force me to live, because I shall look for you on land and sea, and in the very sky if I can reach there. This I beg of you, my dear—do not flee from me."[14] In other words, he believes that she has been brought back to life by a divine power that had taken her away. When he had gone to the tomb, he had had no doubt that she was dead.

In the somewhat later work of Xenophon of Ephesus there is a similar case of disappearance from the tomb. Perilaus has discovered Anthia insensible and, he presumes, dead after taking a strong but not, as it turns out, lethal dose of poison. Laid out in her tomb, Anthia eventually comes to life and regrets that she has been cheated of the death by which she had hoped to join her beloved Habrocomes, whom she, for her part, believed to be dead.[15] But just as in Chariton some pirates learn that the newly buried Anthia has been accompanied by a considerable supply of gold and silver, and so they enter the tomb and carry her off with the treasure. Thus Perilaus, an eminent personality of the region, who had been in love with Anthia, becomes inconsolable upon discovering that the body has vanished from the tomb.[16] Unlike Chaereas in Chariton, the canny Cilician immediately interprets the empty tomb as a sign of body snatching, although it later becomes clear that the supposedly dead Anthia is indeed alive. In both stories the opened and empty tomb is an essential stage in ensuring the survival of the heroine. A credulous lover, in one

14. *Ibid.* 3.3.7.
15. Xen. Eph. *Ephes.* 3.8.
16. *Ibid.* 3.9.

case, infers a divine resurrection, and a more worldly lover, in the other, opts for theft of the corpse.

For what seems at first an unequivocal resurrection we must look to the novel of Achilles Tatius, in which the heroine, Leucippe, dies—or seems to die—no fewer than three times. The multiple deaths of Leucippe and the dramatic resurrections that follow them certainly count among the most memorable episodes in the entire novel. If the patriarch Photius is really the author of an epigram in the *Palatine Anthology* about this novel, it is clear that he was as much impressed as anyone:[17]

> The acid taste of love combined with chastity
> Is pictured in the tale of Cleitophon.
> Chaster still the all-astounding heroine:
> Leucippe beaten, shaved, and much abused.
> But, most astounding!—she endured three executions.

All three executions constitute high drama. They are elaborately stage-managed productions. In the first episode the notorious bandits of the Egyptian Delta, known here and elsewhere as the Boukoloi ("cowherds," "rangers"), carry out a sacrifice of Leucippe in the sight of the narrator.[18] They pour a libation over her head and lead her around an altar while a flute makes music and a priest intones something sacral in Egyptian.[19] She is then laid out on her back and tied to stakes in the ground, presumably upside down, since her position is compared to that of Marsyas attached to a tree in the old story of the competition with Apollo. A member of the sacred band plunges a sword into Leucippe's

---

17. *Anth. Pal.* 9.203. The stylish translation is by J. Winkler, in B. P. Reardon, ed., *Collected Ancient Greek Novels* (1989), p. 174, n. 10.

18. Achill. Tat. *Leuc. and Cleit.* 3.15–17. For the Boukoloi, see Chapter II above, *ad fin.*

19. *Ibid.* 3.15.3: ὁ ἱερεὺς ᾖδεν, ὡς εἰκός, ᾠδὴν Αἰγυπτίαν.

heart and saws all the way to her abdomen so that the entrails burst out. All her internal parts are then divided up solemnly and eaten by the bandits in a ceremony of rustic communion. Soon after witnessing this horrifying spectacle, the narrator receives from an approaching friend the astonishing news, "Leucippe will now come to life again."[20] The narrator is understandably incredulous, whereupon the friend taps several times on the top of the coffin into which the remains have been placed. A voice is heard from beneath the lid; and, when the coffin is opened, Leucippe rises up to embrace her beloved even though her stomach is, embarrassingly, still gaping wide open.

Achilles Tatius favors the reader with a detailed account of the organization of this miraculous episode as if it were a scene in the theater. An animal hide stuffed with bloody entrails was attached to Leucippe's stomach, and so on. The sword that penetrated deep into her was a trick sword in which the blade returned into the hilt as it was pressed against the body. The whole affair was managed, we learn, by a professional stage actor with an expertise in simulation worthy of the Grand Guignol. Both death and resurrection were apparent, not real. But they were, it must be admitted, memorable theater.

A few books later Leucippe dies again in another grotesque and gruesome episode, in which her head is cut off.[21] Yet only a little after that her beloved receives a letter from Leucippe in which she writes to him long-sufferingly that she has died twice. He asks a friend, "Has Leucippe come to life again?"[22] The answer is patently yes. The third death and resurrection are perhaps a little less sensational but equally false. This time they

20. *Ibid.* 3.17.4: Λευκίππη δέ σοι νῦν ἀναβιώσεται.
21. *Ibid.* 5.7.4: ἀποτέμνει αὐτῆς τὴν κεφαλήν.
22. *Ibid.* 5.18.4 (τέθνηκα ἤδη δεύτερον), 5.19.2 (Λευκίππη πάλιν ἀνεβίω;).

involve a report of death conveyed by a jealous lover to Leucippe's true love, the narrator, Cleitophon.[23]

In the Latin novel of Apuleius, the *Metamorphoses,* what appears in the Greek romances about death and resurrection is elevated to a major theme. This work, about the transformation of a man into an ass and his eventual repatriation to the human state and conversion to the worship of Isis, is clearly based on a lost Greek novel.[24] Death and resurrection, both literal and symbolic, may well have been very important in the original Greek work, but there is no doubt that for Apuleius it was an essential representation of the transition to spiritual fulfillment. Communication with the dead, necromancy, and visits to the Underworld are all conspicuous in Apuleius's novel (with echoes of the *Odyssey*),[25] and these, of course, represent the more traditional forms of returning from the grave.

In the exquisite myth of Cupid and Psyche, descent into the Underworld and return from it are literal facts of the narrative, whereas in the history of the man-turned-ass known as Lucius they are figurative. Once Lucius achieves his fulfillment under the auspices of Isis, in the eleventh book of the novel, he declares, "I have approached the confines of death and, having once trodden upon the threshold of Proserpina, I have made my return, traveling through all the elements of the world."[26] During the regrettable period in which he had the form and behavior of an ass,

23. *Ibid.* 7.1.4, 6.

24. Cf. B. E. Perry, *The Ancient Romances* (1967), pp. 211–35, on the *Metamorphoses* by Lucius of Patrae.

25. Cf. Apul. *Met.* 9.13: "nec inmerito priscae poeticae divinus auctor apud Graios summae prudentiae virum monstrare cupiens multarum civitatium obitu et variorum populorum cognitu summas adeptum virtutes cecinit."

26. *Ibid.* 11.23.

Lucius recognized that his family and slaves all thought that he was dead, so that, when they finally saw him alive again, they truly believed that he had been resurrected. This is, for Apuleius, a kind of symbolic rebirth, which he describes in Book 10 by a remarkable phrase. There a dead child rises from its coffin into his father's waiting arms by a process Apuleius calls *postliminium mortis*.[27] *Postliminium* is a technical term from Roman law: it concerns the rights of a Roman citizen who is captured by the enemy and, by virtue of his being a captive, has the legal position of a slave. Yet the right of *postliminium*, the *ius postliminii*, allowed the captive, after his return from captivity, to recover all his former rights as if he had never been captured at all.[28] Apuleius's transference of this term to the restoration of the dead to life equates death with the servility of a captive and life with the restoration of full citizen rights. This appears to be the only example of such a Roman interpretation of death and resurrection, but it is a powerful one and entirely worthy of the great African writer and rhetorician who conceived it.

The religious or quasi-religious implications of death and resurrection in other fiction of the Roman imperial age emerge clearly enough from the biography of the sage and wonder worker Apollonius composed by the sophist Philostratus in the early third century at the request of the empress Julia Domna. Among Apollonius's many miracles is a case of resurrection, which, as Philostratus tells it, is not to be understood as an apparent death or *Scheintod*. Nor is it to be understood as simply symbolic. After all, Philostratus makes the pretense, throughout his biography of Apollonius, that this is a well-documented account according to

27. Ibid. 10.12; cf. 2.28: ("corpusque istud postliminio mortis animare"), 3.24 ("in meum Lucium postliminio redibis").

28. T. Mommsen, *Römische Staatsrecht*, 3d ed. (1887) vol. 3.1, pp. 656–57, n. 1, and pp. 831–32.

the record of a certain Damis, one of Apollonius's own companions. That claim is in all probability part of the larger fiction of the work, but it is certainly worth noting that, within the framework of the claim, there is no mechanical explanation of the supernatural occurrence. A girl at Rome, from a distinguished family of consular rank, had died just at the time of her wedding. During the elaborate funeral ceremony, with all the lamentations over an unconsummated marriage (as Philostratus wryly observes), the sage Apollonius appeared and said peremptorily, "Put the coffin down. I will stop you crying for the girl." He then asked the name of the girl, touched her, spoke quietly to her, and she woke up as if from a sleep and returned to her father's house.[29] Philostratus recalls at this point the story of Alcestis brought back to life by Heracles, although it is by no means comparable. Of Apollonius, Philostratus remarks that he may perhaps have seen a spark of life in the deceased, which the doctors had not noticed, or he may indeed have revived and restored her life when it had been snuffed out. "The true explanation of this has proved unfathomable," writes Philostratus, "to me no less than to the bystanders." We are left in doubt as to whether this is a case of resuscitation or resurrection, but the miraculous element prevails.

A century after Philostratus the pagan Hierocles, in his tendentious work against Christianity modeled on the great diatribe of Celsus, found in the miracles of Apollonius, not surprisingly, a powerful pagan parallel for the miracles of Jesus Christ.[30] Certainly the parallel with the miracle of Jesus at the city called Nain, as recounted in Luke, cannot be missed.[31] When Jesus came to the gate of the city, a dead man was being carried out, the only son of his mother, who was a widow. And

29. Philost. *Vit. Apoll.* 4.45.
30. See above, Chapter IV, n. 49.
31. Luke 7.12–15.

the people of the city were thronging around her. He told the mother not to weep, "and he came and touched the bier: and they that bare him stood still. And he said, 'Young man, I say unto thee, Arise.' And he that was dead sat up and began to speak. And he delivered him to his mother." Both Philostratus and Luke presented these stories as part of a narrative in the form of history, ἐν εἴδει ἱστορίας, to use the emperor Julian's phrase.[32] But whether either recorded an episode that actually happened remains unclear. What *is* clear is the close similarity of the stories, for which no parallels can be found before the mid-first century A.D.

Taking resurrection seriously in a polytheist world was not confined to inspirational or quasi-religious narratives such as the *Life of Apollonius.* Philostratus himself has given us a memorable example of mythological revisionism in his dialogue the *Heroikos,* in which the various rectifications of Homer are introduced by none other than a resurrected hero, Protesilaus.[33] This famous man had been a Greek from Thessaly in the expedition against Troy, who fulfilled a prophecy by stepping first on the soil of Asia Minor and dying immediately thereafter.[34] His memory was cherished through the ages, not least by Alexander the Great, who sacrificed to him on his own journey to the East, a sacrifice that was commemorated in turn in the second century of the Christian era in Arrian's narrative of Alexander's campaign.[35] Protesilaus seems to have been a popular figure in the literature of later Greece and of Rome. A story had grown up that he had left behind a bride whom he had recently married, and he was therefore allowed to join her from the Underworld for a

32. Julian, *Epist.* 89b, 301b (Bidez).
33. Philost. *Heroik.* p. 130, ll. 17–32 (Kayser).
34. Herod. 9.116–20.
35. Arrian, *Anab.* 1.11.15.

few hours in return for his patriotic death.[36] But this inversion
of the Alcestis and Orpheus stories nonetheless remained firmly
within the old tradition of returning from the Underworld.
What appears in the period from Nero onwards, however, is
a Protesilaus who is actually alive again and talks amiably to
people in the Troad. The vineyard worker who explains all this
to his amazed visitor from Phoenicia says calmly that Protesilaus
lives and converses with him about the history of the Trojan War
on regular occasions. As we have come to expect, Homer and the
post-Homeric cyclic poems are shown to be wrong in many
particulars. Philostratus's presentation of the resurrected Protesilaus was scarcely original with him. Already in Chariton the
unhappy Dionysius of Miletus cries out, "What Protesilaus is
this, who has come back to life to plague me?"[37] And in the
writings of the second-century orator Aelius Aristides, whose
career falls between Chariton and Philostratus, we read that it is
known that Protesilaus now associates, after so many centuries,
with the living (μετὰ τῶν ζώντων).[38] Protesilaus is not only
himself the vehicle for revising the Homeric stories. He has been
revised so as no longer to be part of any old-fashioned legend like
that of Alcestis or Orpheus. He is resurrected bodily, mingles
with the people of the Roman empire, and instructs them as a
teacher his disciples.

This new image of Protesilaus with a second life (rather than
simply accorded a brief tryst with his wife) first shows up in our
extant literature from antiquity in Petronius's novel, the *Satyricon*. Encolpius, whose inability to perform sexually is an im-

---

36. See Philost. *loc. cit.* (n. 33 above). Note also C. C. Vermeule,
"Protesilaos," *NM* 38 (1992), 341–46.
37. Chariton, *Chaer. and Call.* 5.10.1: Ποῖος οὗτος ἐπ' ἐμοῦ
Πρωτεσίλεως ἀνεβίω;
38. Ael. Arist. *Orat.* 3.365 (Behr; *Orat.* 46 Dindorf).

portant part of the last set of the surviving fragments of the novel, considered that he was effectively dead in that part of his body where once he had been an Achilles: "funerata est illa pars corporis, qua quondam Achilles eram."³⁹ When finally he is restored and able to display his old prowess before an amazed Eumolpus, he declares that you would think him more lucky (*gratiosiorem*) than Protesilaus or any of the other ancients ("quam Protesilaum aut quemquam alium antiquorum").⁴⁰ This is, of course, a generalized reference to those who returned from the dead, but the choice of Protesilaus for particular mention is surprising and striking. He is the polytheists' new representative of bodily resurrection. And for Encolpius, in particular, resurrection becomes a metaphor for erection.

The widespread use of the resurrection motif in many forms of Roman imperial fictional writing—erotic romance, hagiography, mythological revisionism, and satire—suggests an unusually great interest in this subject, far beyond any interest documented for earlier periods. It even shows up in the theater, in the most surprising circumstances. As Jack Winkler perceptively pointed out more than a decade ago,⁴¹ the sober and genial Plutarch recorded with great respect his admiration for a performer who could simulate death perfectly and thereby astound the audience by his visible return to life. What is so remarkable about the performer that Plutarch saw is that he was a dog.

"He gave a fine performance of various actions and emotions required by the plot, and in particular, when they experimented on him with a supposedly deadly poison (which in the plot turned

---

39. Petron. *Satyr.* 129.1.

40. Ibid. 140.12. I am grateful to W. S. Anderson for emphasizing to me the proper sense of *gratiosiorem*.

41. J. Winkler, "Lollianus and the Desperadoes," *JHS* 100 (1980), 155–81, esp. 173–75 on *Scheintod*.

out to be merely a sleeping potion), he took the bread soaked in poison and, after gulping it down, he began in a moment to shudder and misstep and let his head sag down. Finally he lay stretched out on the ground like a corpse and let them drag his body and carry him around as the plot of the drama required. And, when he noticed his cue in certain words and movements of the actors, he first began to stir gently, as if waking up from a deep slumber, and then, raising his head, he looked around. To the wonder of the audience he then got up and went to the right actor and fawned on him, wagging his tail and showing all the signs of canine affection. Everyone was thrilled, even the emperor, for the aged Vespasian was present in the audience."[42] This is quite clearly a canine version of the scenes that are familiar to us from the Greek novels. The date of the incident is worth noting—the last years of the emperor Vespasian, in other words, about ten years after the death of Nero and in the lifetime of both Ptolemaeus Chennus and Antonius Diogenes.

With all this interest in resurrection, it is no wonder that a strict polytheist like the anti-Christian Celsus viewed the apparent success of Jesus Christ in raising the dead, to say nothing of the bodily resurrection of Jesus himself, in a larger context. Even Origen, in beginning his refutation of Celsus's work, acknowledges that the mystery of the resurrection, "because it has not been understood," is talked about and ridiculed by the unbelievers.[43] In his *True Doctrine* Celsus had expressed profound skepticism about Jesus's raising of the dead as well as about Jesus's own resurrection. He obviously said or implied that the raising of Lazarus was a piece of fiction, inasmuch as Origen is obliged to reply to him in these terms. Here are Origen's words:

42. Plut. *De Soll. Anim.* 973e–974a.
43. Origen, *Contra Celsum* 1.7: ἀλλὰ καὶ μὴ νοηθὲν τὸ περὶ τῆς ἀναστάσεως μυστήριον θρυλεῖται γελώμενον ὑπὸ τῶν ἀπίστων.

"That he really did raise the dead, and that this is not a fiction [πλάσμα] of the writers of the Gospels, is proved by the consideration that, if it was a fiction [πλάσμα], many would have been recorded to have been raised up, including people who had already been a long time in their tombs. But, since it is not a fiction [πλάσμα], those of whom this is recorded may easily be enumerated."[44] He then mentions Lazarus and one or two other examples. This is perhaps not one of Origen's strongest arguments.

When he turns to Jesus's own resurrection, Celsus clearly reflects the fascination and the skepticism of his age. If his contemporary Marcus Aurelius could say, in his philosophic way, that a human being had within him the resources for living again, he probably referred to spiritual regeneration, but he used the very language of resurrection that is familiar from the novelists— ἀναβιῶναί σοι ἔξεστιν.[45] A more flamboyant philosopher and another contemporary of Celsus, Peregrinus Proteus, actually did manage to achieve bodily resurrection after his fiery demise on a funeral pyre at Olympia. Or so, at least, a serious and reliable old gentleman (Lucian calls him ἀξιόπιστος) reported. Peregrinus after death appeared before him garbed in white and crowned with olive.[46] There is an unmistakable echo here of the Gospel narratives, although the white clothes belong in that story to the angelic messenger or messengers who proclaim the risen Christ. In the earliest account, that of Mark, Mary Magdalene

44. *Ibid.* 2.48.
45. Marc. Aur. *Ad Se Ipsum* 7.2, on which see R. B. Rutherford, *The Meditations of Marcus Aurelius: A Study* (1989), p. 180.
46. Lucian, *Pereg.* 40. For a recent treatment of the *auto-da-fé*, see C. P. Jones, "Cynisme et sagesse barbare: Le cas de Pérégrinus Proteus," in *Le cynisme ancien et ses prolongements,* ed. M.-O. Goulet-Cazé (1993), pp. 305–17, esp. pp. 311–13.

and two other women encounter a young man in Jesus's tomb clothed in a long white garment.[47]

The scene at the tomb after the crucifixion must, in fact, have made a powerful impression on far more than the followers of Peregrinus. There had never been anything like it before, and not even Peregrinus's ancient prototype, the Indian Brahman Calanus, had intimated, as it turned out, that he would join Alexander in the flesh. The meeting in Babylon betokened, as we have seen, Alexander's death, not a new life for Calanus.[48] Yet from the mid-first century onward the empty tomb and all that it implies becomes a conspicuous theme in both Chariton and Xenophon of Ephesus. Chariton wrote of Chaereas, for example, "When he reached the tomb, he found that the stones had been moved and the entrance was open. He was astonished at the sight and overcome by fearful perplexity at what had happened."[49] This is not much removed from the words of Mark: "They came to the tomb at sunrise, and they said to one another, 'Who will roll away the stone for us from the entrance of the tomb?' Looking up, they saw that the stone was already rolled away . . . , and they were frightened."[50]

The novelistic interest in empty tombs and the fictional possibilities of tomb robbing bears directly upon the interpretation of a notorious Greek inscription acquired a little over a century ago by a European collector in France from a Palestinian antiquities dealer. The stone, for which no precise provenance can be given, must nonetheless come from somewhere in or near Judaea. Its inscribed text is in Greek, but it is demonstrably a

47. Mark 16.5.
48. See above, pp. 102–3, on Cicero, *De Div.* 1.47.
49. Chariton, *Chaer. and Call.* 3.3.1–2: εὗρε τοὺς λίθους κεκινημένους . . . ὁ μὲν οὖν ἰδὼν ἐξεπλάγη.
50. Mark 16.3–5: ἀνακεκύλισται ὁ λίθος . . . καὶ ἐξεθαμβήθησαν.

translation from a lost Latin original. That original was an edict of an unnamed Roman emperor on penalties to be established for breaking open and violating tombs. The letter forms of the inscription suggest a date in the middle or late first century A.D.[51]

Obviously the implications of such a text from Palestine at this time, so soon after the fateful disappearance of Jesus's body from his tomb, have been apparent from the beginning. Some have even, on that account, suggested a modern forgery. But as Louis Robert and others have insisted, the stone must be accepted as a genuine document.[52] The evidence of Chariton and Xenophon can now serve to reinforce the epigraphical and linguistic arguments in placing this imperial edict in the Neronian or immediately post-Neronian context. The novelists' interest in this ghoulish topic may well duplicate the preoccupations of the emperor who issued the edict—whatever we may suppose those preoccupations to have been. Christianity could indeed have been involved. The designation of the edict as διάταγμα Καίσαρος, without specification of the emperor's name, is probably a reflection of a *damnatio* that precluded an exact reference. If so, this will be a ruling of either Nero himself or of Domitian.

The accumulated evidence points to the power of the Gospel stories about Jesus's resurrection for anyone, like Celsus, who wished to deny their credibility. Celsus knew the old myths of returning from the Underworld, but he was perfectly capable of distinguishing these from the actual resurrection in the body. For that, he was inclined to believe there must have been some kind

51. L. Robert, *Collection Froehner, vol. 1, Inscriptions grecques* (1936), pp. 114–15.

52. *Ibid.* 115: "La thèse de L. Zancan, selon qui l'inscription serait un faux fabriqué entre 1864 et 1878, est proprement absurde. Cet érudit a montré seulement qu'il ignore tout de l'épigraphie grecque. C'est une chose assez répandue que l'ignorance de l'épigraphie."

of trickery or stage machinery, as so often in the novels. "How many others produce wonders like this," asked Celsus, "to convince simple hearers whom they exploit by deceit? They say that Zamolxis, the slave of Pythagoras, also did this among the Scythians, and Pythagoras himself in Italy. . . . They say that Orpheus did this among the Odrysians, and Protesilaus in Thessaly, and Heracles at Tinerum, and Theseus. But we must examine this question, whether anyone who really died ever rose again with the same body."[53] That was clearly the crucial point for Celsus. In his opinion, those who saw the resurrected body, with its marks of the crucifixion, were only a hysterical female and one or two others equally deluded.

Origen is obliged to labor long and hard in refuting this point. For Celsus, as Origen admits, the old heroic stories about the men who descended to Hades and came back or brought women back with them are essentially fantastic tales. Accordingly, Jesus's resurrection from the dead cannot be compared with them.[54] Yet that is precisely Celsus's point. Nor is Celsus likely to have been the first to elaborate it. In the hundred years before he composed his treatise, it is obvious, as our review of the literature amply demonstrates, that the theme of bodily resurrection was all too familiar to pagan readers and even audiences in the theater. For a sage like Apollonius or for a hero like Protesilaus, a resurrection of this kind could be presented in total seriousness and enjoyed, if not necessarily believed. The fiction has its own truth, which carried conviction within its context. But in most narratives it is obvious that episodes of resurrection in the flesh had to be explained as the inevitable result of a false or apparent death, a *Scheintod*. Thus the death could not be credited, nor the resur-

53. Origen, *Contra Celsum* 2.55.
54. *Ibid.* 2.56.

rection. It was undoubtedly some such perspective as this that Celsus brought to his reading of the Gospels.

The question we must now ask is whether from a historical point of view we would be justified in explaining the extraordinary growth in fictional writing, and its characteristic and concomitant fascination with resurrection, as some kind of reflection of the remarkable stories that were coming out of Palestine precisely in the middle of the first century A.D. Already in the days of the emperor Claudius the name of Jesus Christ was known at Rome.[55] The Gospels, as we have them, had not yet been written, but much of the story that they were to contain was obviously already in circulation. By the time of Claudius's successor, the emperor Nero, that great philhellenic patron of the arts, the claims of the Christians were being widely disseminated at Rome as a result of the residence of Paul in the city and the infamous immolation of many Christians in the aftermath of the fire that consumed it in 64.[56] By this time it is possible that the earliest of the extant Gospels was actually being written. If the nature of contemporary fiction helps us, as it does, to explain the interpretation that Celsus brought to the Gospels, it would be wise next to consider the possibility that the Gospel stories themselves provided the impetus for the emergence of that fiction in the first place.

---

55. Suet. *Claud.* 25.4 (*impulsore Chresto*). This early second-century reference to a report of Christ not very long after his death betrays a confusion between Χριστός and χρηστός, which probably reflects an oral transmission of the story at that time.

56. Cf. Tac. *Ann.* 15.44.2–5.

CHAPTER SIX

Polytheism and Scripture

For those who have been raised in the ambiance of one of the great monotheist religions—Judaism, Christianity, or Islam—polytheism poses far more problems than its multiplicity of gods. Both the centrality and the diversity of the rituals of polytheism, extending from the domestic environment to the grandest civic ceremonies, suggest that religious education and religious practice were essentially one and the same thing for pagans. Children were not instructed in polytheism apart from their introduction to established rites and participation in them. Worshippers turned to no sacred texts that they found either inspirational or inviolate. Stories of the gods, from Homer to the latest mythographers, were read and appreciated, but scarcely canonical. Polytheism had, in short, no scripture.

The absence of religious texts, as opposed to philosophical reflections on religion (such as we find in Plato, Aristotle, or Cicero), moved Arnaldo Momigliano to observe in an important passage in one of his later writings, "The mere fact that one had to study in order to be pious is a strange notion which made Judaism increasingly intellectual—not what cults were known for in the Graeco-Roman world. . . . We should recognize that, while in Athens and Rome thinking about religion usually made people less religious, among Jews the more you thought about religion, the more religious you became." Had he lived longer, Momigliano would probably have addressed the interesting question of whether the increasing pagan awareness of monotheism, as mediated by Christianity in Greek texts, had some kind of resonance in pagan literature. The aretalogies and encomia of the greater Greek and Roman deities never became universal texts for the devout. These were genres for expression of individual, personal piety. As Momigliano recognized, one could hardly expect devotional texts from polytheist authors, in view of the essentially ritualistic rather than intellectual character of their religion. But some parallel to the monotheist scriptures might well be expected eventually in a world in which monotheism and polytheism were approaching a direct and momentous collision.[2]

It was the literary critic Northrop Frye, reflecting on the nature of biblical narratives, who suggested that what became known in modern times as the romance constituted nothing less than a secular scripture. The stories of the romantic novels, with their fiery emotions, strong loves and hates, hair-raising vicissitudes, exotic settings, and memorable incarnations of great virtue and great vice bore many resemblances to the biblical narratives. Although ancient fiction was not a primary concern of Frye's, he quite properly included several works of the genre as forerunners

---

1. A. Momigliano, "Religion in Athens, Rome, and Jerusalem in the First Century B.C.," *Annali della Scuola Normale Superiore di Pisa,* ser. 3, 14 (1984), 873–92, citation from the final page. This article was reprinted in *Ottavo contributo alla storia degli studi classici et del mondo antico* (1987), pp. 279–96; in *On Pagans, Jews, and Christians* (1987), pp. 74–91; and (in Italian translation) in *Saggi di storia della religione romana* (1988), pp. 27–43.

2. For a powerful analysis of the impact of this collision, see now G. Fowden, *Empire to Commonwealth: Consequences of Monotheism in Late Antiquity* (1993).

of the romance as secular scripture. He outlined his theories in a series of Charles Eliot Norton Lectures at Harvard.[3] Coincidentally, only a few years later, again in a series of Norton lectures, Frank Kermode also turned to the Bible, and in particular to the New Testament, to develop a sophisticated analysis of novelistic elements in the Gospels.[4] He argued that the problem of historical truth is so elusive in the Gospel narratives that those accounts are better viewed simply as fiction with a semblance of truth. The meaning and, obviously, the inspirational value of works of this kind do not depend upon their historical veracity, although apprehension of that meaning nonetheless does depend upon a provisional or temporary belief in their veracity. This is, in Kermode's words, a "benign deceit" that readers even today continue to countenance. "How far we do so," observes Kermode, "because of the saturation of our culture by the Gospels and traditional interpretations one need not try to say."[5]

Both Frye and Kermode, from their separate literary perspectives, offer something like a solution to the dilemma posed by Momigliano, even though Momigliano wrote later than they did. The material in the Gospel narratives, as well as in the Acts of the Apostles, constituted a kind of narrative fiction in the form of history (ἐν εἴδει ἱστορίας, as Julian was to say)[6] that was essentially new to the Graeco-Roman world. Its roots belonged in the inspirational narratives of the Hebrew Bible. But the written versions of these narratives, and presumably oral versions that preceded them, were disseminated among Greeks and

3. N. Frye, *The Secular Scripture: A Study of the Structure of Romance* (1976).

4. F. Kermode, *The Genesis of Secrecy: On the Interpretation of Narrative* (1979).

5. *Ibid.* 122.

6. Julian, *Epist.* 89b, 301b (Bidez).

Hellenized Jews. Their availability in the Greek language gave them a far greater impact in the Graeco-Roman world. Their potential for stimulating secular narratives grew with the portentous diffusion of Christian doctrines and practices as outlined by the evangelists. All this was set in motion in the generation after the crucifixion of Jesus, which, it will be recalled, occurred in the latter part of the reign of Tiberius.

⟨Parallels in form and substance between the writings of the New Testament and the fictional production of the imperial age are too prominent to be either ignored or dismissed as coincidental.⟩Both Celsus, in his attack on the Christians, and Origen, in his defense of them, recognized the similarities, particularly, as we have seen, where apparent miracles—such as the open tomb or resurrection of the dead—were at issue.[7] It is, furthermore, a plain fact of chronology that the distinctive fictional forms of the Roman empire begin, on present evidence, no earlier than the reign of Nero and proliferate conspicuously soon thereafter. To be sure, antecedents of this fiction, such as the Homeric tales, Ctesias's Persian fantasies, Xenophon's *Cyropaideia,* Hellenistic travel literature, and the lost lubricities of the short Milesian tales, serve to identify some of the scattered elements that the imperial writers assimilated, brought together, and transformed in order to create what, on any accounting, was a wholly new phenomenon in Graeco-Roman literature.[8] Let us remember that the invocation of sources and antecedents never provides an expla-

7. See Chapter V above.

8. For antecedents, see, for example, B. E. Perry, *The Ancient Romances: A Literary-Historical Account of Their Origins* (1967), or the more recent and more sophisticated book by B. P. Reardon, *The Form of Greek Romance* (1991). For possible Eastern antecedents, G. Anderson, *The Novel in the Graeco-Roman World* (1984).

nation of an innovation: they can only reveal, inadequately at best, some of the building blocks that were used to construct it.

If the implied contacts between polytheist fiction and Christian scripture are suggestive, and if the chronology of the two is remarkably similar, we may be emboldened to press Northrop Frye's concept of the secular scripture a little further. Achilles Tatius's novel, *Leucippe and Cleitophon,* provides a good point of departure. Near the beginning of the second book we are in the city of Tyre at a feast of Dionysus Προτρύγαιος ("of the Vintage," "of the Harvest of Grapes").[9] The writer declares that Dionysus is considered one of the gods of the city, and he pauses to tell the story of the origin of the feast. It is nothing less than an account of the discovery of wine: "No wine ever existed among men before the Tyrians had it," says Achilles Tatius, although he soon reveals that he is aware of the well-known, rival tradition among the Athenians that the god brought wine first to a certain Ikarios in Attica.[10] What follows is a story that is attested nowhere else, neither in the mythographic tradition nor in any of the detailed accounts of Tyrian legends such as we find in the *Dionysiaca* of the poet Nonnos.

Before the arrival of Dionysus in Tyre everyone drank water; but, when the god found himself hospitably received by a shepherd, he offered as a pledge of friendship a cup with a delectable red drink. "Where, stranger," said the shepherd, "did you find this water stained with red? Where did you find such sweet blood? For nothing of the kind flows on the ground." After the shepherd offered an eloquent paean to the bouquet of the wine, Dionysus proclaimed solemnly, "This is the water of early autumn, this is the blood of the grape [τοῦτό ἐστιν ὀπώρας ὕδωρ,

9. Achill. Tat. *Leuc. and Cleit.* 2.2.1.
10. *Ibid.* 2.2.2–3.

τοῦτό ἐστιν αἷμα βότρυος]." He then took the shepherd to a vine, plucked a cluster of grapes, and crushed it before him, saying, "This is the water, and this is the fountain."[11]

No reader acquainted with the evangelists can miss the similarity to the Christian eucharist. Some have also seen a hint of the Johannine miracle at Cana, where Jesus turned water into wine. But, since the wine here is pressed directly from the grape, the eucharistic parallel is more compelling. In a footnote to his recent and brilliant translation of Achilles Tatius, the late Jack Winkler observed, "If the resemblance of Dionysus's words and gesture to the Christian eucharistic rite is not accidental, it must surely be interpreted as parody."[12] Yet in the rich texture of Achilles Tatius's novel, parody is an element so hard to find that it would be rash to invoke it here. On the other hand, the parallelism is hardly likely to be accidental. The language is far too close, and the solemnity of the divine gift to mortal men too marked. Observe the phrasing in the Gospel of Matthew, for example: τοῦτό ἐστιν τὸ σῶμά μου and τοῦτο γάρ ἐστιν τὸ αἷμά μου—"This is my body," "This is my blood."[13] The connection between Achilles Tatius in this passage and the account of the eucharist in the Gospels has, it must be said, been exploited by some exegetes of the New Testament, but in a very curious way. The novelist is assumed to provide reliable evidence about an otherwise unknown rite in Phoenicia in the vicinity of Tyre. That rite is then advanced, on this basis, as a pagan precedent for the utterance of Jesus before his

11. *Ibid.* 2.2.4–6.

12. J. Winkler in B. P. Reardon, ed., *Collected Ancient Greek Novels* (1989), p. 192 n. 25. Note that in his translation Winkler rearranged the text of Book 2 of Achilles Tatius. He placed chapters 2 and 3 between chapters 8 and 9.

13. Matt. 26.26, 28.

disciples.[14] Jesus is seen, in other words, as reworking an old pagan tradition in the formulation of his eucharistic program. This is a reckless way to handle evidence that belongs indisputably to a time at least a century or so after the lifetime of Jesus. The tendency of Christian interpreters to look for the pagan origins of Christian rites, utterances, and images has all too often obscured influences in the reverse direction. This is particularly true for late antiquity, but to some extent also for the earlier imperial period. The story of the eucharist had, by the time of Achilles Tatius, been available in all the canonical Gospels as well as Saint Paul's First Letter to the Corinthians. We know from the famous letter of the younger Pliny to the emperor Trajan, as well as from ecclesiastical texts, that the story of the eucharist and the rite enjoined by Jesus had led to disreputable reports, culminating in accounts of Thyestian banquets among the Christians.[15] Partaking of divinity by eating human flesh and drinking human blood was not a familiar occurrence to the Greeks and the Romans. In the immemorial past the gods had done this once or twice among themselves (Kronos being the most notorious example, thought by many scholars to come from a pre-Hellenic tradition), and the horrors of Thyestes' table symbolized the practice. In recalling the boiled dinner that Tantalus served from the pieces of his son, Pelops, Pindar had to admit that he found it hard to call any of the blessed ones a cannibal (γαστρίμαργος).[16] Such

14. For a learned presentation of this kind of interpretation, see Morton Smith, "On the Wine God in Palestine," *Salo Wittmayer Baron Jubilee Volume,* American Academy for Jewish Research (1975), pp. 815–29.

15. Cf. Pliny, *Epist.* 10.96, and Euseb. *Hist. Eccles.* 5.1.52 (martyrs of Lyon): ἡμεῖς δὲ οὔτε ἀνθρώπους ἐσθίειν. . . .

16. Pindar, *Olymp.* 1.52: ἐμοὶ δ' ἄπορα γαστρίμαργον μακάρων τιν' εἰπεῖν· ἀφίσταμαι.

a thing was plainly alien to him. Nor, for that matter, was this practice any more familiar to the Jews, for whom the drinking of blood of any kind was strictly forbidden and the eating of human flesh inconceivable.[17]

Achilles Tatius therefore invented something new and exciting when he transferred the revelation of wine from Attica to Tyre. The most plausible source for his invention is the Gospel story. It makes far more sense to postulate a direct influence upon the Greek novelist than to suppose that the writer innocently preserved an otherwise unknown tradition of great antiquity that was the source that inspired Jesus himself. Ikarios in the old account of the discovery of wine and the Tyrian shepherd in the new one play similar roles, but the hieratic pronouncement of Dionysus, as it is given in Achilles Tatius, has absolutely no parallel in the versions of the Ikarios story from earlier times. The formulation τοῦτό ἐστιν—"This is . . ."—is unique in this text.

Of course, the most surprising thing about the eucharist is the miracle of the body and blood of Jesus Christ. Not even Dionysus is made to say that the wine is actually his blood. As Margaret Visser has recently observed in her book *The Rituals of Dinner* with reference to the eucharist, "The ultimate taboo is reverently broken as the people share out and consume his [i.e., Jesus's] body and blood, the proofs of his love."[18] Theologians have long speculated about the origins of the eucharist. Not surprisingly they have found it a singularly intractable topic. When the *Reallexikon für Antike und Christentum* reached the letter E, the editors prudently postponed action by instructing the reader who looks up *Eucharistie* to turn instead to *Kultmahl*, an item that

17. Cf. M. Smith, *Jesus the Magician* (1978), pp. 122–23.
18. M. Visser, *The Rituals of Dinner* (1991), p. 36.

has not yet appeared. The eucharist is celebrated on the occasion of Passover, but as Gillian Feeley-Harnik has observed in her important book *The Lord's Table,* the Jewish Passover is an affirmation of family and nation, whereas the eucharist and Last Supper affirm the annihilation both of family ties and of national allegiance.[19] Insofar as food serves as a language for expressing human relations, the totally unexpected and unprecedented admonition to eat flesh and drink blood symbolizes, according to Feeley-Harnik, an inversion of the Jewish Passover ceremony.[20] Certainly there is nothing in traditional Judaism that would explain what Jesus was doing at the Last Supper. As we have already observed, drinking blood was taboo; and, as Morton Smith has trenchantly remarked, the rites of Judaism did not include cannibalism.[21]

But if the origins of the eucharist remain controversial, the way in which nonbelievers perceived it is less so. The underlying concept of the eucharist would appear to be nothing less than cannibalism. As Margaret Visser says, it is treated as a rite of the highest solemnity and reverence, but it is nonetheless a breaking of the ultimate taboo. To the extent that anthropologists can help, some conclusions can be drawn— and have been drawn—from the actual rather than miraculous (or symbolic) practice of cannibalism. In one of its forms, notably among the Aztecs, the eating of human flesh that has been dedicated and sacrificed to a god allows the cannibalistic worshipper to become one with that god. This point is made well, and with reference to the Christian rite, by Peggy Reeves Sanday in her study *Divine Hunger: Cannibalism as a Cultural*

19. G. Feeley-Harnik, *The Lord's Table: Eucharist and Passover in Early Christianity* (1981), chap. 5 ("The Last Supper").
20. Ibid. 130.
21. See n. 17 above.

System.[22] She rightly draws attention to the occasional reappearance of this motif in some of the Christian martyr literature. For example, when the body of the dead Polycarp is borne from the fire in which his corpse was merely baked rather than burned up by the flames, masses of people rush forward to have a share in his holy flesh (κοινωνῆσαι τῷ ἁγίῳ αὐτοῦ σαρκίῳ).[23]

< Cannibalism, like resurrection, was utterly alien to traditional Graeco-Roman life and thought. > Before the first century of the Christian era it figures very rarely in texts of any kind apart from a few myths such as those of Kronos or Thyestes. Only the adventurous and ever-curious Herodotus seems to show any sympathetic interest whatever in the subject. He treats it three times, in connection with remote peoples on the edge of the inhabited world. Of the Massagetae, who were neighbors of the Scythians, he records that it was customary for relatives to cook and eat an elderly member of the family who had recently died (unless of disease).[24] This endocannibalism, as the anthropologists call it, is well attested in other societies and should not be discredited in Herodotus. The same form of cannibalism is also reported for a tribe called the Padaeans, east of the Indians (and therefore about as far away as any people Herodotus talks about).[25] The Issedonians, another people beyond the Scythians, likewise eat their relatives but are careful to cook the flesh together with that of a sheep, which is specially sacrificed at the time of the person's decease.[26] The two meats are mixed together

22. P. R. Sanday, *Divine Hunger: Cannibalism as a Cultural System* (1986), p. 193.
23. *Martyr. Polyc.* 17.
24. Herod. 1.216.
25. Ibid. 3.99.
26. Ibid. 4.26. On eating one's dead relations, see also the remarks

and served up indiscriminately at a banquet, in much the same way as was done in African Mali until relatively recently, according to still-unpublished reports from an anthropologist who has been working there.[27]

Herodotus's three accounts of cannibalism are all confined to the eating of relatives or tribespeople, in a rite designed to ensure the cohesion and continuity of family or nation. There is no trace whatever of anything like the Aztec union with the divine through cannibalistic sacrifice and ceremony. And, apart from Herodotus, there is scarcely any trace of the practice at all until the Christian era. Morton Smith has suggested that cannibalism, real or metaphorical, may have played some role in magical practices of the Hellenistic and early Roman periods, but the evidence is extraordinarily tenuous. In two papyri wine is imagined to be blood in an invocation designed to induce love in the person for whom the spell is cast. For example, "Give blood of Osiris that he gave to Isis to make her feel love in her heart for him, give to cause her to feel a love for him in her heart, the love that Isis felt for Osiris."[28] This sort of thing may, or may not, have some connection to the mystery cults of the imperial period, but in the case neither of magic nor of the mysteries do we find the clear motif of cannibalism that dominates the eucharist. The magical parallels were, of course, important for Morton Smith in trying to prove his famous and eccentric case that Jesus was actually a Palestinian magician of the period. But, even if we

---

of the Stoic Chrysippus, preserved in Sextus Emp. *Pyrr. Hyp.* 3.247–48, a reference for which I am indebted to A. A. Long.

27. I have this information through the courtesy and generosity of Prof. Sarah Brett-Smith.

28. Smith (n. 17 above), pp. 122–23, citing *The Demotic Magical Papyrus of London and Leiden* (1904), XV.

reject that case (as most do), there is no clear explanation to put in its place.

Although we do not know exactly what the origins of the eucharist were, we do know that nothing like it had been seen before. That is a major reason why the origins are so hard to find. Certainly no ritual cannibalism, documented, alleged, or metaphorical, had ever appeared within the societies confined by the Graeco-Roman world. It is in the Gospel of the most intellectual and subtle of the evangelists, John, that we can see clearly that the eucharistic rite posed substantial difficulties even for the people to whom Jesus brought his message. John acknowledged candidly that the Jews murmured against Jesus because he said, "I am the bread that came down from Heaven." Not unreasonably the Jews asked, "Don't we know his father and mother?" And they went on to ask, "How can this man give us his flesh to eat?"[29] We can hardly doubt that the eucharist was a startling innovation in the Graeco-Roman world. It is hardly surprising that, as word of it spread, tales arose of Thyestian banquets and worse.

Accordingly, when we find cannibalism playing a very conspicuous role in imperial fiction, it is no more likely to be there accidentally than the proclamation of Dionysus about the blood of his grape. The Boukoloi, the "rangers" or "desperadoes" of the Nile Delta, are the chief but by no means only exhibit. In the first of the three executions of Leucippe in Achilles Tatius's novel, we read that the Boukoloi tied the heroine up and that one of them "next raised a sword and plunged it into her heart and sawed all the way down to her abdomen. Her viscera leaped out. The attendants pulled out her entrails and carried them in their hands over to the altar. When it was well done they carved the

29. John 6.41–52.

whole lot up, and all the bandits shared the meal."[30] Leucippe's lover, Cleitophon, who watched the whole episode, observed with a rueful and epigrammatic pun, "The burial [ταφή] of your entrails is now the nourishment [τροφή] of the bandits." Or, as Winkler has wittily rendered this in his translation, "Your insides are inside the outlaws, victuals in the vitals of bandits."[31]

There is a comparable scene of cannibalism in the fragment of the Phoenician novel ascribed to a certain Lollianus and published a little over twenty years ago by Albert Henrichs.[32] A boy is thrown on his back, his heart cut out and placed over the fire. Then someone removes it, cuts it in half, sprinkles it with barley, and drizzles a little olive oil over it. When it is adequately cooked, we read that the heart is distributed to the participants. The parallelism in the motif of cannibalism has led some to assume that the villains here must again be the Boukoloi or Egyptian rangers, but obviously that inference is by no means necessary.[33] The subject seems to have acquired a certain vogue in the time of Lollianus and Achilles Tatius.

It surfaces again, for example, in a more conspicuous and better-known text, the *Toxaris* of Lucian, that memorable exploration of cultural relativism in the Roman empire. The allusive and well-read Lucian is probably evoking the reports in Herodotus when he makes his Greek speaker in the dialogue say to the Scythian interlocutor, "I should not have expected friendship to be so highly cherished among the Scythians . . . , judging

30. Achill. Tat. *Leuc. and Cleit.* 3.15.4–5.

31. Winkler (n. 12 above), p. 217.

32. A. Henrichs, *Die Phoinikika des Lollianos* (1972), translated by G. N. Sandy in B. P. Reardon, ed., *Collected Ancient Greek Novels* (1989), pp. 810–12.

33. Cf. Henrichs (n. 32 above), pp. 48–56 ("Die Anthropophagie der ägyptischen Bukolen").

by all that we hear about them, and especially the report that they
eat their dead fathers."³⁴ It is immaterial that it was not exactly
the Scythians who did this, but their neighbors. What is significant is the presence of the item at all, presumably borrowed, if
inaccurately, from Herodotus.

Nor was Lucian the only one who found such long-neglected
information in Herodotus now of particular interest. Petronius
was the earliest of the fictional writers of the imperial age, so far
as we can tell, to introduce the theme of cannibalism and, in the
process, to recall both Herodotus and the Christian eucharist.
Unlike Achilles Tatius, Petronius was a parodist, and a brilliant
one. His extraordinarily nuanced treatment of the eating of
human flesh occurs in the last extant fragments of the *Satyricon*,
where someone is reading out the testament of Eumolpus and
then commenting on it.³⁵ It may be that this is Eumolpus himself
in anticipation of his own death, or perhaps it is one of his eager
legatees after he has died, or perhaps he has died a death that is
to turn out only make-believe, a *Scheintod*. We have no way of
telling.

But the text of the testament of Eumolpus is unambiguously
preserved and of exceptional interest. It reads as follows: "All
those who are legatees in my will, apart from my freedmen, shall
take what I have given only under the following condition—that
they divide my body into parts and eat it in the presence of the
assembled people."³⁶ The recitation of the will continues, in our
extant text, "We know that among certain tribes this practice is

34. Lucian, *Tox.* 8. Cf. *De Luctu* 21. For Herodotus, see above in
this chapter, with reference to Herod. 1.216, 3.99, 4.26.

35. Petron. *Satyr.* 141.2–4.

36. Ibid. 141.2. A century later Artemidorus mentions a dream
(*Oneir.* 5.42) in which cannibalism portends inheritance of the property of the victim.

still maintained, that the dead should be consumed by their relatives, maintained indeed to such a degree that the sick are frequently blamed because, by living on, they are diminishing the quality of their flesh. With this in mind, I advise my friends not to refuse what I order, but to eat my body [*corpus*] with the same enthusiasm with which they have cursed my spirit [*spiritum*]."37

The reference to complaints about the sick in a cannibalistic society seems manifestly to derive from Herodotus's account of the Padaeans, of whom he says, "If one of their number be ill, man or woman, they take the sick person, and, if he be a man, the men of his acquaintance proceed to put him to death, because, they say, his flesh would be spoiled for them if he pined and wasted away with sickness. The man protests he is not ill in the least; but his friends will not accept his denial—in spite of all he can say, they kill him, and feast themselves on his body. So also, if a woman be sick, the women who are her friends take her and do with her exactly the same as the men."38 Eumolpus clearly views the legacy hunters, the *captatores*, as the equivalent of the resentful Padaeans waiting for their sickly tribesman to die. But

37. Petron. *Satyr.* 141.3–4. The text of the last sentence in K. Müller's edition is "his admoneo amicos meos ne recusent quae iubeo, sed quibus animis devoverint spiritum meum, eisdem etiam corpus consumant." In *CQ* 37 (1987), 529–32, G. B. Conte proposes *devorarint* for *devoverint*. The pleonasm *devorarint/consumant* weakens the sentence, and *spiritum devorare* seems an odd expression (it would appear to be unexampled, and it is certainly not the same as "devouring" words or books, for which examples can be produced). The contrast of *spiritus* with *corpus* is vital here: one cannot consider both edible.

38. Herod. 3.99, cited by K. Müller in the apparatus to *Satyr.* 141.4 in his edition. For the possibility that what we find in Herodotus may reflect an ancient τόπος, cf. H. D. Rankin, "Eating People Is Right: Petronius 141 and a ΤΟΠΟΣ," *Hermes* 97 (1969), 381–84.

why, we must ask, has Petronius recalled a Herodotean item of
this kind? Why has he made Eumolpus compose his will in this
bizarre way? There is, after all, nothing about a will in Herodotus, nor indeed in any of the three Herodotean reports of
cannibalism. How did Petronius come to conceive of a *testamentum* like this? For a *testamentum* is what this is.

When Jesus spoke to his disciples at the Last Supper, he
invoked a covenant according to which his disciples were to share
in his body and blood by consuming bread and wine. In the Greek
Gospels this is made explicit by the use of the Greek word
διαθήκη. In Matthew, "This is my blood, of the covenant [τῆς
διαθήκης]." In Mark, "This is my blood," again τῆς διαθήκης.
In Luke, "This cup is the new covenant [διαθήκη] in my blood,"
and essentially the same words are used by Paul in addressing the
Corinthians.[39] The new translations of the Bible regularly use the
word "covenant" to render διαθήκη, but it was not always so.
The King James version, which had so tremendous an influence
on English literature afterward, used the translation "testament." And that is why the New Testament is called the New
Testament. In Greek, it is simply the new διαθήκη—"the new
covenant."

In fact, the translators of the King James version were accu-
rately reflecting the normal meaning of διαθήκη in the Greek of
Jesus's own time. It was the word for "testament" or "will,"
whereas only in the context of Hellenistic Judaism was it a word
for "covenant."[40] It is fair to say that the sense "testament" was

39. Matt. 26.28, Mark 14.24, Luke 22.20, I Cor. 11.25.
40. See *Theologisches Wörterbuch zum Neuen Testament* vol. 2
(Stuttgart, 1935) p. 127, s.v. διαθήκη, for the normal usage in Greek:
"Weitaus am häufigsten *letztwillige Verfügung, Testament,* term. techn.
der griech. Rechtssprache aller Zeiten, aber auch der Schriftsteller- und
Volkssprache geläufig." For the transition to "covenant" in Hellenistic

accordingly far more general than the sense "covenant." Greek speakers to whom Christian doctrine was unfamiliar would certainly have heard in these phrases the word for "testament" or "will," and understood in Jesus's instructions to eat and drink the testamentary stipulations of a man about to die. The word διαθήκη must have been current in Greek accounts of the Last Supper from the death of Jesus onward. This is guaranteed by the consistent and uniform use of the term when the various Gospel narratives were finally written down.

Since, as the *Oxford English Dictionary* guarantees, the word "testament" in English is just as unfamiliar in the sense "covenant" as it was in Greek, the ordinary English reader can have a good sense of how the Gospel text in Greek must have sounded to a Greek reader by simply listening to the words of the King James translators. Matthew: "For this is my blood of the New Testament." Mark: "This is my blood of the New Testament." Luke: "This cup is the New Testament in my blood." And so on. Of course, in more recent times, the very expression "New Testament" means, first and foremost, the aggregate of scriptural texts that we call the New Testament. But, if we can think away that association and hear the word "testament" in its normal sense, we shall have some understanding of what a Greek heard in διαθήκη.

The testament or "covenant" is called new, καινή. This word too has particular connotations that differentiate it from the normal word for "new" in Greek, νέος or, in the feminine, νέα. Καινότης, "newness," implies and often means "innovation," something radically new and different, even strange.[41] The

---

Judaism, by way of the Septuagint in renderings of Hebrew *berīt*, see ibid. 128–31.

41. Ibid. vol. 3 (1938), pp. 450–53, s.v. καινός, καινότης. For

Καινὴ Διαθήκη, therefore, is something altogether new and different in the way of a testament. It may be suggested that the brilliant parody of Petronius makes play with this sense of "New Testament" in giving us the highly innovative, not to say strange, will of Eumolpus. It would be stranger still if the stipulation that his legatees eat his body were not a pointed allusion to the Gospel story of the Last Supper. The distinction he makes between his *corpus* and his *spiritus* reflects perfectly the opposition of σάρξ (or σῶμα) and πνεῦμα in the Gospels.[42] That is to say, Petronius has given us the New Testament of Eumolpus. He then goes on through the mouth of a speaker (who may even be Eumolpus himself or someone else) to justify the terms of the will by recalling the practices of northern barbarians together with a few alleged cases of cannibalism in time of war and under the pressure of imminent starvation.

Petronius's treatment of this motif is not only the most brilliant in extant fiction but also, as we have observed, the earliest. Like so much else in the history of imperial fiction, it dates from the reign of Nero. It was a portent of the impact that the tales of the evangelists were to have on the imagination of writers and readers in the Graeco-Roman world for several centuries to come. The Gospels were themselves supplemented by the ac-

---

standard Greek usage (p. 450): "νεός . . . das, was noch nicht da war, was erst vor kurzem entstanden oder in der Erscheinung getreten ist; dagegen καινός das, was im Vergleich zu anderem neu und eigenartig ist . . . , verschieden von dem Gewohnten, daher Eindruck machend."

42. Cf. Matt. 26.41: τὸ μὲν πνεῦμα πρόθυμον, ἡ δὲ σάρξ ἀσθενής (also Mark 14.38). For σάρξ (σῶμα) vs. πνεῦμα generally, see W. Bauer, K. Aland, and B. Aland, *Griechisch-deutsches Wörterbuch zu den Schriften des Neuen Testaments und der frühchristlichen Literatur,* 6th ed. (Berlin, 1988), cols. 1356–57.

count of the Acts of the Apostles, a work that in small compass already strikingly resembles the novels of the polytheists.[43] The structure and pace of the book of Acts would still be the envy of any novelistic writer today. It begins with an ascension, moves briskly to the grisly death of a treacherous disciple, and then turns smartly to a scene in which tongues of flame produce a babble of many languages. For invention and exotica, this is hard to beat. The narrative continues across a broad geographical canvas that includes Syria, Phoenicia, Cyprus, the Pamphylian coast, Asia Minor, Macedonia, and Greece. It includes dramatic courtroom scenes and rises to a climax in a richly described episode of shipwreck that is worthy to stand alongside the many shipwrecks in pagan fiction.

Yet, as the popularity of the novelists grew—and the papyri increasingly suggest that it did—it was perhaps not surprising for the Christians to pick up in turn and to exploit the very genre that seemed to have come into being, to some degree, as a response to stories of theirs that were now enshrined in the canonical Gospels. By the early third century at the latest, the Christians, to our knowledge, had acquired at least one major novel of their own along the lines of the polytheist ones and in evident imitation of them.[44] In this work, known only from excerpts, some in the

---

43. For a useful study of parallels, R. I. Pervo, *Profit with Delight: The Literary Framework of the Acts of the Apostles* (1987). Unfortunately, Pervo sees novels as an influence on Acts—which is implausible for chronological reasons. R. A. Burridge, *What Are the Gospels? A Comparison with Graeco-Roman Biography* (1992), p. 245, finds Pervo unconvincing from the perspective of genre. No one seems to have asked whether Acts, whatever its genre, could itself have influenced the novelists. Once again we have the familiar failure to look for the impact of Christianity on polytheist culture.

44. For a still useful, general account of this work, see Perry (n. 8

Greek original and some in Latin translation, a Roman matron takes her twin sons away to Athens after being warned in a dream that all three of them would perish if they remained. One son remains behind with his father, and that boy is called Clement, destined to be a saint. The father loses all contact with his wife and twin sons; he assumes that they have met their deaths. But he nonetheless determines to go off on a voyage to find out the truth. Young Clement, now on his own, makes his way to Jerusalem and there encounters Saint Peter, who edifies him by a series of at least twenty sermons. Peter and Clement, together with other disciples, then go to an island off the coast of Phoenicia to see the sights and, in doing so, encounter an old woman begging in front of a door. The old woman turns out ultimately to be Clement's mother, who reveals that her husband's brother had once made sexual advances to her, and it was really this that had decided her to leave Rome. Subsequently the twin brothers turn up at Syrian Laodicea under false names, and finally the father, as an old man, turns up as well.

There can be no doubt, nor has there been, that this is a Christian novel, closely parallel to the polytheist novels apart from the addition of Peter's homilies. The work is now known as the *Clementine Recognitions,* or, more pedantically and quite unnecessarily, the *Pseudo-Clementine Recognitions.* The title reflects various discoveries (ἀναγνωρίσεις) of the whole family of Clement in the course of the novel and also reflects the Latin name, *Recognitiones,* attached to the collection of excerpts known in Latin translation. The *Clementine Recognitions* may be said to constitute the meeting of Christian and secular scrip-

---

above), pp. 285–93. See also W. Heintze, *Der Clemensroman und seine griechischen Quellen* (1914); and O. Cullmann, *Le problème littéraire et historique du roman Pseudo-Clémentine* (1930).

ture. They represent the appropriation, probably the inevitable appropriation, of a pagan and popular genre that itself owed so much to the miraculous narratives, both oral and written, of the early Christians. Fiction became antiquity's most eloquent expression of the nexus between polytheism and scripture.

The emergence of martyrologies, beginning in the second century, soon made more novels like the *Clementine Recognitions* superfluous. The martyr narratives were to provide the basis for an abundant production of instructive fiction in the centuries ahead, although the earliest martyr acts, based as they were on carefully maintained protocols of interrogation, had rather more historical veracity than was to be characteristic of the genre later.[45] The fecundity of hagiographical narrative may even have inspired the latest of the pagan novelists, Heliodorus. At least it should be said that his account of Charicleia on the burning pyre could easily fit into a saint's life: "Charicleia climbed onto the pyre and positioned herself at the very heart of the fire. There she stood for some time without taking any hurt. The flames flowed around her rather than licking against her; they caused her no harm but drew back wherever she moved toward them, serving merely to encircle her in splendor."[46]

The great novelists evidently appealed to Christians as much as pagans. They lost none of their appeal, even in late antiquity. If after the fourth century there were few (or none) to practice

45. For an examination of the early martyr acts from this point of view, see G. W. Bowersock, *Martyrdom and Rome*, The Wiles Lectures (Queen's University of Belfast), forthcoming (Cambridge University Press).

46. Heliod. *Aeth.* 8.9.13. Cf., e.g., *Martyr. Polyc. 15:* "For the flames, bellying out like a ship's sail in the wind, formed into the shape of a vault and thus surrounded the martyr's body as with a wall. And he was within it not as burning flesh."

this craft any more, the works of Achilles Tatius, Heliodorus, and others continued to be read. Julian disliked them, but in his literary taste he was as atypical of his age as he was in most things. He had a horror of the erotic. The Christians, fortunately, did not, and the novelists, no less fortunately, seem to have avoided including material that was directly offensive to Christians (unless, of course, such material was censored in transmission—which is most unlikely). In any case, the Christians made these pagan works their own by piling fiction upon fiction. They were able to legitimize the novels and to ensure their survival until the time when the patriarch Photius could, with some surprise, peruse them. Heliodorus was declared to have been a bishop, and so was Achilles Tatius.⁴⁷ More remarkable still was the early Byzantine appearance of a saint whose parents turned out to be none other than Leucippe and Cleitophon.⁴⁸ Nothing could be farther from the truth than to say, as Ramsay MacMullen has, that Christianity put an end to a taste for novels.⁴⁹ For a long period there were no new novelists, because the hagiographers took their place. But the extant novels continued to be read and prized.

It is easier to explain the gradual disappearance of a certain kind of creativity than it is to speculate on what promoted it in

47. Heliodorus: Socrates, *Hist. Eccles.* 5.22 (cf. Niceph. Call. *Hist. Eccles.* 12.34). Achilles Tatius: *Suda* s.v. Ἀχιλλεὺς Στάτιος (*sic*).

48. St. Galaktion, son of Leucippe and Cleitophon: Migne, *PG* 116.93. Cf. Perry (n. 8 above), p. 346, n. 4.

49. R. MacMullen, "What Difference Did Christianity Make?" *Historia* 35 (1986), 322–43, esp. 342: "There were demonstrable changes in literature, too. Nothing similar to Heliodorus', Apuleius', or Petronius' novels could be published, nor poetry like Catullus' or Ovid's. *There* was a difference!" This article was reprinted in the author's *Changes in the Roman Empire: Essays in the Ordinary* (1990), pp. 142–55, with the passage cited here on pp. 154–55.

the first place. But in the course of these six chapters the connection between imperial fiction of various kinds and the Gospel narratives has grown ever stronger. The stories of Jesus inspired the polytheists to create a wholly new genre that we might call romantic scripture. And it became so popular that the Christians, in turn, borrowed it back—in the *Clementine Recognitions* and in the massive production of saints' lives. For the centrality of fiction in the history of the Roman empire, the debate between Celsus and Origen across nearly a century provided the first and principal clues. Celsus was, after all, a child of the second century, and he framed his questions in accordance with the thinking of that age. And it is not only Celsus's contemporary Lucian who authorizes us to generalize from the work of Celsus in this way. It is the simple fact that Origen essentially accepted the same premises as Celsus in trying to refute his arguments.

When narrative fiction made a triumphant return to the Greek world in the twelfth century, it did so by explicitly echoing the work of the earlier masters. The authors of the entry "Romance" in the new *Oxford Dictionary of Byzantium* say of this late Byzantine fiction, "Why the romance should reappear at this moment, after six centuries, is a question yet to be answered satisfactorily."[50] Byzantinists of today are just beginning to address this question in earnest. If fiction can be seen not only within its historical context but as a part of the historical continuum itself, an answer should soon be at hand. One may be allowed to suspect that, in the vast and subtle theological writings of Byzantium in its final centuries, another Origen or even another Celsus may be found to point the way.

50. E. M. and M. J. Jeffreys, *Oxford Dictionary of Byzantium*, ed. A. Kazhdan, vol. 3 (Oxford, 1991), p. 1804.

Artemidorus, *Oneir.* 1.56

Only a year after Roger Pack published his Teubner
edition of the *Oneirocritica* of Artemidorus in 1963, Toufic Fahd
produced the text of an Arabic translation of this work from the
Sultan's library in Istanbul. Although the translator did not
always fully comprehend the Greek in front of him, it is usually
possible to deduce what his Greek text looked like, thus providing a witness considerably earlier than the two manuscripts
(V and L) on which Pack had been obliged to rely. For the Arabic
version dates, in the opinion of virtually everyone, to the great
days of translation at Baghdad in the ninth century.

In responding to this new witness, as well as to reviews of both
his own edition of the Greek and of Fahd's of the Arabic, Pack
acknowledged the dramatic impact upon the study of Artemidorus: "On Artemidorus and His Arabic Translator," *TAPA* 98
(1967), 313-26; and "Artemidoriana Graeco-Arabica," *TAPA*
106 (1976), 307-12. Since the Arabic version now clears up
several difficulties in a passage that is relevant to the argument
in the first chapter of the present book, it would seem desirable
to lay out the evidence here. It has not been assembled before.

Oneir. 1.56 as printed by Pack in 1963, p. 63, l.15 – p. 64,
l.1:

τραγῳδεῖν δὲ ἢ τραγικὰ ἔχειν δράματα ἢ ἀναπλάσματα
ἢ τραγῳδῶν ἀκούειν ἢ ἰαμβεῖα λέγειν μεμνημένῳ μὲν

146 Appendix A

τῶν εἰρημένων κατὰ τὴν περιοχὴν τὰ ἀποτελέσματα
γίγνεται, οὐ μεμνημένῳ δὲ ταλαιπωρίαι καὶ δουλεῖαι καὶ
5 μάχαι καὶ ὕβρεις καὶ κίνδυνοι καὶ εἴ τι τούτων δεινότερον
ἢ ὠμότερον·τοιούτων γάρ εἰσιν αἱ τραγῳδίαι μεσταί. τὸ δὲ
κωμῳδεῖν ἢ κωμῳδῶν ἀκούειν ἢ κωμικὰ ἔχειν
ἀναπλάσματα ἢ βιβλία, τὰ μὲν τῆς παλαιᾶς κωμῳδίας
σκώμματα καὶ στάσεις σημαίνει, τὰ δὲ τῆς καθ᾽ ἡμᾶς
10 κωμῳδίας τὰ μὲν ἄλλα ἴσα τῇ τραγῳδίᾳ σημαίνει, τὰ δὲ
τέλη χρηστὰ καὶ ἀγαθὰ ὑπαγορεύει· τοιαῦτα γάρ εἰσιν αἱ
ὑποθέσεις τῶν κωμικῶν δραμάτων.

This passage appears in Arabic in Toufic Fahd, *Artémidore
d'Éphèse—Le livre des Songes,* Institut Français de Damas
(1964), p. 117, l. 12 – p. 118, l.8. By a regrettable slip Fahd
omitted a substantial chunk of the Arabic text in this section, as
Franz Rosenthal noted (*JAOS* 85 [1965], 142, quoting the miss-
ing words from the manuscript). Fortunately the words that
Rosenthal has restored do no more than reassure us that the
translator did not actually omit anything. The rendering (of lines
3–4, from κατά to οὐ μεμνημένῳ, inclusive) is unproblematic.

The Arabic can serve to correct Pack's Greek text at four
points.

1. Line 1, τραγικὰ ἔχειν δράματα ἢ ἀναπλάσματα. Contrary to his normal (and reasonable) instinct in preferring V to
L, Pack adopted the reading of L here in printing ἀναπλάσματα.
He evidently did so because V and L agree in ll. 7–8 in κωμικὰ
ἔχειν ἀναπλάσματα, although it is difficult to fathom what Pack
thought the word could mean in either place. In a paraphrase in
TAPA 106 (1976), 309, he wrote of "scenes," which seems inad-
missible philologically as well as hard to construe with ἔχειν in the
obvious sense of "possess." The Arabic renders the whole phrase
by "possess a book of recitation pieces or a book of fabrication
[*sanāʿa*] of poetry." Apart from the equation, made repeatedly,

of tragedy with recitation and the assumption that verse is in question, it is absolutely clear that the translator saw πλάσματα and rendered it literally. When he saw ἀναπλάσματα, as he did in the later line (where both extant independent manuscripts have it), he translated *dalīl,* another literal rendering.

2. Line 4, δουλεῖαι. Both V and L have ἀπολίαι, and Pack had opted for Hercher's conjecture. But the Arabic gives ʿanāʾ ("troubles, misery") at this point and proves Hercher wrong. Pack, in *TAPA* 106 (1976), 309, proposed ἀγωνίαι, despite objections that he candidly acknowledged. But if we remember the frequent interchangeability of o and ω in later Greek and the pertinence of this fact for orthography, we can see at once that V and L have the right word after all. It is simply ἀπωλεῖαι (or ἀπωλίαι).

3. Lines 7–8, κωμικὰ ἔχειν ἀναπλάσματα ἢ βιβλία. Here the Arabic translator certainly had ἀναπλάσματα, but apparently not ἢ βιβλία. His version is "possess a [comic] representation [*dalīl*] in a book [*fī kitābi*]." Now, as we have already observed, ἀναπλάσματα makes little sense here, and the parallel with the lines on tragedy would suggest the disjunction δράματα ἢ πλάσματα. The words ἐν βιβλίῳ, if that is what the Arabic translator saw, must have been a gloss to explain πλάσματα. Reiske had already proposed deleting ἢ βιβλία in V and L for that reason. The gloss would have come when δράματα had fallen out, perhaps creating the prefix ANA in the process: ⟨ΔΡΑΜΑΤΑΗ⟩ΠΛΑΣΜΑΤΑ.

4. Line 9, σκώμματα καὶ στάσεις. This is the reading of L, whereas V has σκώμματα καὶ ταραχὰς καὶ στάσεις καὶ αἰσχρολογίας. The Arabic has clear correspondences for the first three nouns in V, and only for these (*al-madhmūma wa-l-iḍtarāb wa-l-khusūma*). The word αἰσχρολογίας must represent a gloss on these three terms that found its way into the text between the translator's manuscript and V.

The *Aethiopica* of Heliodorus

The discovery of papyri has pushed back the chronology of the extant novels to dates far earlier than those contemplated by Erwin Rohde in his still valuable *Der griechische Roman und seine Vorläufer* (third edition, 1914). Most of the novelists known to us now appear to have written in either the first or the second century A.D.[1] One, however, is evidently of a later date. The fifth-century ecclesiastical historian Socrates identifies him with none other than a bishop in Thessaly at the time of Theodosius I.[2] His novel was alleged to represent a literary indiscretion from the author's benighted early years. Most scholars have refused, perhaps a little too hastily and indignantly, to countenance this identification; but, equally, most have admitted that the novel of Heliodorus, known as the *Aethiopica*, was composed in either the third or the fourth century. Curiously this was the date to which Rohde had also assigned it, although he believed that it was among the first of the ancient novels rather than, as it now appears to be, among the last.[3]

1. Cf. the individual introductions to the translated texts in B. P. Reardon, ed., *Collected Ancient Greek Novels* (1989).

2. Socrates, *Hist. Eccles.* 5.22, 51.

3. E. Rohde, *Der griechische Roman und seine Vorläufer*, 3d ed. (1914), p. 496.

As long ago as 1919 Carlo Conti Rossini, a specialist in the antiquities of Ethiopia, drew attention to a striking parallel between the account of a grand celebration held by the king of Meroe for allies and friends, as described in the tenth book of the *Aethiopica*, and the triumphal procession of Aurelian in 274 A.D., as described in the *Historia Augusta*.⁴ The narrative of Heliodorus, although set long ago in the sixth or early fifth century B.C., seemed in some way to mirror the contemporary world of the author in suggesting close and friendly relations between Meroe and Aksum in the celebration in Book 10. Rohde had unfortunately and injudiciously denounced Heliodorus as representing an impossible liaison: "die Reiche von Meroe und Auxomis haben überhaupt nie gleichzeitig nebeneinander existiert, wie sich unser Dichter es vorstellt."⁵ Conti Rossini knew better. The kingdom of Aksum proclaimed its monarchs on coinage of the third century A.D.⁶ At that time the kingdom of Meroe was still in existence, although Aksum was the rising star. By the middle of the fourth century Meroe had declined into total obscurity. But the concurrence of the two in the third century was enough to excite Conti Rossini's interest in Heliodorus's allusion and, to his eyes, to give some plausibility to the appearance of people from Aksum in the procession of Aurelian along with Blemmyes and Seres, who are similarly on show in Heliodorus's Meroe.

Half a century later, in an important paper on the Greek novels, Jacques Schwartz once again observed the parallels between the tenth book of the *Aethiopica* and the life of Aurelian

4. C. Conti Rossini, "Meroe ed Aksum nel romanzo di Eliodoro," *Rivista degli Studi Orientali* 8 (1919/20), 233–39.

5. Rohde (n. 3 above), p. 484.

6. S. Munro-Hay, *Azania* 14 (1979), 26–27; and 19 (1984), 136; id., *The Coinage of Axum.* (1984).

in the *Historia Augusta*.[7] It is important to remember that, when he wrote, the date of the *Historia Augusta* itself was still hotly contested. For Schwartz and many other scholars, van der Valk and Colonna had succeeded in proving that the novel of Heliodorus must have been written after 350 A.D. Schwartz said that van der Valk had proven the *terminus post quem* "d'une manière irréfutable."[8] Accordingly a reflection of Heliodorus's work in the *Historia Augusta* served effectively to support the late fourth-century dating of the imperial biographies.

The matter was taken up again, from the perspective of Aksum, by Johannes Straub in the *Historia-Augusta-Colloquium* for 1972/74 in his article "Aurelian und die Aksumiten," a paper that he also presented to the Fourth International Congress of Ethiopian Studies at Rome at about the same time.[9] Straub emphasized, with solid arguments, that the international role of the people of Aksum, implied by their presence in Aurelian's triumph, belonged in all probability to the later fourth or fifth century. Because he was concerned with the place of the kingdom within the structure of a literary panegyric, the actual date of Heliodorus's novel was of less importance to him than it had been to Schwartz. But, by a strange irony, only a few years after Straub wrote, the date of Heliodorus's novel was called seriously into question by the Hungarian scholar Tibor Szepessy in two contributions, the later repeating the earlier at greater length.

7. J. Schwartz, *AC* 36 (1967) 549–52.

8. Ibid. 549, citing M. van der Valk, "Remarques sur la date des Éthiopiques d'Héliodore," *Mnemosyne* 9 (1941), 97–100; also to the same effect and better argued, A. Colonna, *Athenaeum* 38 (1950), 79–87.

9. J. Straub, *HA Colloquium* 1972/74 (Bonn, 1976); also in *Quarto congresso internazionale di studi etiopici*, Accademia Nazionale dei Lincei, Quaderno 191 (Rome, 1974), 55ff.

Szepessy's first piece, "Die Neudatierung des Heliodorus und die Belagerung von Nisibis," appeared in 1975, to be followed one year later by a much longer piece, "Le siège de Nisibe et la chronologie d'Héliodore."[10] Szepessy's arguments found considerable favor in the new *Cambridge History of Classical Literature.* The author of the bibliographical appendix there declared unequivocally that Szepessy "has now demonstrated" that Heliodorus belongs to the third century rather than the fourth.[11] If this were to be true, then the *terminus* that Heliodorus provided for the *Historia Augusta* would disappear. Although the late fourth-century dating of the *Historia Augusta* seems by now so firmly assured that the loss of this item would have little consequence, the impact of the novel on the author of the *Historia Augusta* would be that much more surprising. The work would have been so remote from him in time.

Accordingly the relation between Heliodorus and the *Historia Augusta* must be addressed on two fronts: (1) the legitimacy of Szepessy's argument for a third-century date, and (2) the nature and extent of the influence of Heliodorus on the *Historia Augusta.* For there is more than has met the eye hitherto. Let us first attempt to dispatch the date of Heliodorus and, in the process, return to the fourth-century date that Schwartz and others had believed van der Valk and Colonna had so decisively demonstrated. Nor should we forget that, before Szepessy wrote, Ru-

10. T. Szepessy, *Actes de la XIIᵉ conférence internationale d'études classiques: Eirene,* Cluj-Napoca 1972 (Budapest, 1975) 279–87; *Acta Antiqua Academiae Scientiarum Hungaricae* 24 (1976), 247–76.

11. E. L. Bowie, in *Cambridge History of Classical Literature* vol. 1 (Cambridge, 1985), p. 884. The remark may, however, be due to Martin Drury, editor of the bibliographical appendix, rather than Bowie. Drury revised considerably the basic material provided by the authors of the articles in the Cambridge history.

dolf Keydell, who knew later Greek better than almost any scholar in this century, had also published a strong defense of the fourth-century date of Heliodorus in the *Festschrift* for Dölger,[12] and Lacombrade had done the same only a few years later.[13] The consensus that Szepessy chose to attack was therefore a formidable one, and it is astonishing that a new generation of scholars has been inclined to accede with such docility to Szepessy's argument. Only J. R. Morgan, in an excellent study of the *Aethiopica* published in 1982, and Pierre Chuvin, in his recent book on the last pagans, have declared themselves firmly unconvinced by Szepessy.[14]

Despite the length of his two treatments of the issue, Szepessy's *Datierung* turns entirely on a confrontation between Heliodorus's description of the siege of the city of Syene in Book 9 and the details of the historical siege of Nisibis in 350 as provided by Ephraem, the Syriac poet, in his hymns against Julian. Van der Valk, Colonna, Keydell, and Lacombrade had all emphasized the description of the siege of Syene and its similarity with the siege

12. R. Keydell, "Zur Datierung der Aethiopica Heliodors," *Festschrift F. Dölger,* ed. P. Wirth (1966), pp. 345–50.

13. C. Lacombrade, "Sur l'auteur et la date des Éthiopiques," *Revue des Études Grecques* 83 (1970), 70–89.

14. J. R. Morgan, "History, Romance, and Realism in the Aithiopika of Heliodorus," *Classical Antiquity* 1 (1982), 221–65, esp. 226 n. 15. Cf. M. D. Reeve's firm endorsement of Colonna (n. 9 above) before Szepessy in *CQ* 18 (1968), 282. See now P. Chuvin, "La date des Éthiopiques d'Héliodore," *Chronique des derniers païens* (1990), pp. 321–25, in support of the second half of the fourth century. (This part of Chuvin's work is omitted from the English translation [1990].) Among those who have followed Szepessy: M. Maroth, *Acta Antiqua Academiae Scientiarum Hungaricae* 27 (1979), 239–45; R. Lane Fox, *Pagans and Christians* (1987), p. 137 with p. 704 n. 52; C. S. Lightfoot, *Historia* 37 (1988), 117–18.

of Nisibis by comparing the close parallels between Heliodorus's text and Julian's detailed descriptions of the Nisibis siege at two points in his panegyrics of Constantius II.[15] In both episodes the siege is carried out by the construction of massive earthworks around the fortification walls of the besieged city, followed by the introduction of water, in one case from the Nile and in the other case from the Mygdonius, into the space between the city's walls and surrounding earthworks. This maneuver was by no means unknown in antiquity, and a comparable siege is described on the Rosetta stone when Ptolemy V tried to take Lycopolis in 196 B.C.[16] But the parallels between Heliodorus's description and the text of Julian are astonishingly close. And in the third and fourth centuries the siege of Nisibis was certainly the great example of the application of this technique. Szepessy undertook to extract from the Syriac texts, although he could not read them in the original, details of the siege (which the saint himself actually lived through), so as to show that the real siege of Nisibis was different in character from the siege of Syene. Hence, Szepessy would have us believe that the future emperor Julian, in his panegyrics of Constantius, was describing something that did not really happen and was doing so by borrowing from a Greek fictional romance. The notion of Julian's borrowing from a work of fiction in official praise of an emperor concerning a recent historical event seems so obviously absurd that it is hard to believe that either Szepessy himself or anyone else could have believed it.

But Szepessy's thesis is not only inherently improbable: his interpretation of the Syriac verses of Ephraem is simply wrong. Once his misconceptions are removed, we are, fortunately, back

15. Heliod. *Aeth.* 9.3f., with Jul. *Or.* 1.22–23 (27b–30b), 3.11–13 (62b–62c) Bidez.

16. *OGIS* 90, 22ff.

where we were in the days of van der Valk, Colonna, and Keydell. Szepessy's analysis had been founded on the nineteenth-century Latin translation of Ephraem's poems published by Bickell at Leipzig.[17] He noticed that, in Bickell's Latin, the Persian king laid siege to Nisibis by building up *tumuli* around it, and he then observed that *tumuli* could scarcely be the same as the earthworks that ringed the city of Syene. So, he said, there were mounds at Nisibis, whereas there was a surrounding dam at Syene: Julian's text quite obviously echoes Heliodorus, and therefore Julian must be mistaken under the influence of Heliodorus's text. This is nonsense, and nonsense that has done much damage. Had Szepessy consulted the modern text of Ephraem by Edmund Beck, published in 1961 (and therefore well before Szepessy wrote),[18] he would have read in Beck's German translation that the word that Bickell had translated as *tumuli* was there rendered *Wälle:* "er richtete die Wälle auf" (*Hymn* 2.9; cf. 1.3). The Syriac word is simply the plural of *tall,* which certainly can mean "a mound" but often, especially in the plural, means "earthworks," as can be seen from the *Thesaurus Syriacus* of Payne Smith, where Latin translations *aggeres* and *moles* are both provided. The Syriac plural *talâla* matches precisely the use of χώματα to describe the earthworks in Heliodorus (9.3), and χώματα is similarly the word used in two places by Julian in his account of the siege of Nisibis (*Or.* 1.27b, 3.62c). So, far from showing that the siege in Heliodorus and Julian is different from the actual siege of Nisibis, Ephraem proves that it is exactly the same. We should, therefore, be able to rest in the calm and well-documented assurance that the novel of Heliodorus was indeed written at some date after 350 A.D.

17. *S. Ephraemi Syri Carmina Nisibena,* ed. G. Bickell (Leipzig, 1886).

18. E. Beck, *CSCO* Scriptores Syri 92 (Louvain, 1961).

With this problem behind us, we may now turn once again to the relation between Heliodorus and the *Historia Augusta* in the life of Aurelian. Hydaspes, the king of Meroe in the story, receives his allies and well-wishers after defeating the Persian king. Notable among those present on this festive occasion are, as we have already observed, the *Axomitae,* who are represented in the highly favorable position of being ὑπόσπονδοι and exempt from the payment of tribute.[19] Also present are Blemmyes and Seres.[20] These last are clearly identified in some way with the Chinese, as the name would suggest, by their presentation of a gift of silk to the Meroitic king. The Aksumites offer a giraffe (καμηλοπάρδαλις). As Conti Rossini, Schwartz, Straub, and others have noticed, this curious conjunction of representatives reappears in Aurelian's triumph of 274, as described in the *Historia Augusta.* In a list in chapter 33 of the life of Aurelian, the Blemmyes and Axomitae (spelled in the Latin text *Exomitae*) are to be found, and later in the same context at chapter 41 the Blemmyes and Exomitae reappear together with the Seres. Furthermore, the first list incorporates a reference to giraffes: *camelopardali* are duly registered. It would be hard to deny that the author of the *Historia Augusta* had been inspired by his reading of Heliodorus to bring these strange bedfellows together.

The appearance of the Seres or Chinese is particularly telling. They clearly have no business being in this part of the world, although the silk trade had led to some confusion between the proper location of the Chinese and their presence or influence in areas of India and the Red Sea. But the placement of Chinese, with gifts of silk, in the region between Aksum and Meroe is almost unique and serves as a guarantee of the interdependence

19. Heliod. *Aeth.* 10.27: φόρου μὲν οὐκ ὄντες ὑποτελεῖς, φίλοι δὲ ἄλλως καὶ ὑπόσπονδοι.

20. Ibid. 10.25–26.

of Heliodorus and the *Historia Augusta*. Only once in the extant literature of antiquity do the Seres appear in a similar location. That is in Lucan's *Pharsalia,* where they are said in Book 10 to live at the sources of the Nile.[21] So Heliodorus was certainly drawing on some kind of authentic ancient tradition that may possibly reflect an indigenous name for people in the region that sounded to outsiders rather like Seres. But the presence of Blemmyes, Axomitae, and *camelopardali* make it certain that the author of the *Historia Augusta* was not drawing on a reading of Lucan (unlikely in any event). His interest in Aksum and the surrounding areas of Ethiopia may well reflect, like the novel of Heliodorus itself, the ascendancy of that kingdom in the fourth century to the position of a major power. As we have seen, the gold coinage of the kings of Aksum in the third century proves that the place was not negligible even before Meroe completely declined. But by the middle of the fourth century, at the time of the conversion of Aezanas to Christianity, Aksum had become a world power with substantial conquests to its credit. These are well documented in famous inscriptions of the king Aezanas himself.[22]

But the connection between the *Aethiopica* and the *Historia Augusta* is not confined to the celebrations of Hydaspes and Aurelian. In the ninth book of the novel Heliodorus provides a detailed description of the famous mailed cavalry in the Persian

21. Lucan, *Pharsal.* 10.292–93. Cf. A. Dihle, "Serer und Chinesen," in *Antike und Orient,* Supplemente zu den Sitzungsberichte, der Heidelberger Akademie der Wissenschaften, Phil.-Histo. Klasse, 2 (1983), pp. 201–15.

22. E. Littmann, "Äthiopische Inschriften," in *Miscellanea Academica Berolinensia* 2.2 (1950), 97–127; L. Kirwan, *Kush* 8 (1960), 163–65. Cf. W. Y. Adams, *Nubia: Corridor to Africa* (1984), pp. 386–87.

army known as κατάφρακτοι. Rome had seen this formidable cavalry several times in the past during its confrontations with the Persians as well as the Parthians. Crassus had met them at the battle of Carrhae, and Constantius had been so impressed by them that he organized a unit of this mailed cavalry within his own Roman army.[23] A new inscription from Bolu in Turkey has now clarified our understanding of the cataphracts by demonstrating that the so-called *clibanarii* noted by Ammianus and the *Notitia Dignitatum* were simply a subcategory of the mailed cavalry, called generally κατάφρακτοι or in Latin *cataphractarii*.[24] The inscription proves as well that there were units of this kind of cavalry already in the Roman army before 324. Constantine or perhaps the Tetrarchs must have introduced this Persian innovation into the Roman military. But there is no doubt that it was particularly important for Constantius, as we know from the panegyrics of Julian, who waxes eloquent on the formidable impression made by the κατάφρακτοι. It is this formidable impression that is conveyed no less vividly in Heliodorus's account of Persian cavalry in Book 9.

The astonishing look of these troops seems to have given rise in the second half of the fourth century to an almost banal

23. Plu. *Crass.* 27; Nazarius, *Pan. Lat.* 4(10).22. See D. Hoffmann, *Das spätrömische Bewegungsheer und die Notitia Dignitatum* (1969/70), vol. 1, pp. 266–67.

24. M. Speidel, *Epigraphica Anatolica* 4 (1984), 151–56. The break in the inscription shown on Speidel's plate 15, taken from E. Pfuhl and H. Möbius, *Die ostgriechischen Grabreliefs*, vol. 2 (1979), p. 334, no. 1041, is a fault in the photograph, not in the stone. I possess, through the courtesy of the late Nezih Fıratlı, a photograph of the stone in perfect condition. In F. Becker-Bertau's edition of the text (*Inschr. Kleinasiens, Claudioupolis* [Cologne, 1968], no. 40), the stone is also presented as broken.

comparison of a mailed warrior to a living statue. For example, in the two references to the cataphracts in his panegyrics to Constantius, Julian compares the cataphracts to statues: καθάπερ ἀνδριάντας, and τὸ κράνος . . . ἐπικείμενον ἀνδριάντος λαμπροῦ, and again ὥσπερ ἀνδριάντες.[25] It is with these parallels in mind that we should read Heliodorus's description of the cataphract as ἀνδριὰς κινούμενος.[26] Ammianus Marcellinus picked up the theme when he wrote that you would think that the *cataphractarii* were *simulacra, non viros.*[27] Only a little later Claudian, in his second invective against Rufinus, declared, *credas simulacra movere / ferrea.*[28] These troops clearly made an impression on writers, and they made it in the second half of the fourth century.

At the battle of Strasbourg in 357, as Ammianus Marcellinus records in detail, the cataphracts played an important role on the Roman side, but unfortunately the Alamanni were able to bring them down by the clever device of having footsoldiers crouch underneath the horses and attack them in the unprotected belly.[29] This maneuver for dealing with the attack of cataphracts was scarcely new: Plutarch records that it was used by Crassus.[30] But the most recent and notorious use of this technique was undoubtedly at the battle of Strasbourg, and consequently this may well lie behind the detailed account of the Blemmyes' successful assault on the Persian cataphracts in Book 9 of Heliodorus's *Aethiopica.* This cunning method of bringing the cataphracts down is described in loving detail in the novel.

25. Jul., *Or.* 1.30 (37c–d), 3.7 (72c) Bidez.
26. Heliod. *Aeth.* 9.15.5.
27. Amm. Marc. 16.10.8.
28. Claud. *In Ruf.* 2.359–60.
29. Amm. Marc. 16.12.22.
30. Plut. *Crass.* 27.

This material on the mailed cavalry points clearly to the later fourth century and finds its reflection in the *Historia Augusta,* first in a passage in the life of Alexander Severus but, for our purposes, most significantly in the life of Aurelian.[31] There they are, paraded in triumph in the same *pompa* that displays the Chinese, the Aksumites, the Blemmyes, and the giraffes. Both Heliodorus and the author of the *Historia Augusta* undoubtedly shared a common contemporary interest in these magnificent warriors. But that they show up together with other peoples who have manifestly been moved in from the novel by Heliodorus suggests that their cameo role in the life of Aurelian was a recognition of their fictional appearance in a recent and exciting Greek novel. The author of the *Historia Augusta* thus paid homage to an older contemporary who revived the art of narrative fiction after some two centuries of neglect.

31. *HA* Alex. Sev. 56.5, Aur. 34.4. Cf. R. Syme, *Ammianus and the Historia Augusta* (1968), p. 41.

Bibliography

Adams, W. Y. *Nubia: Corridor to Africa.* Princeton, 1984.

Anderson, G. *The Novel in the Graeco-Roman World.* London, 1984.

Barnes, T. D. *Constantine and Eusebius.* Cambridge, Mass., 1981.

Bartsch, S. *Decoding the Ancient Novel.* Princeton, 1989.

Bowersock, G. W. *Greek Sophists in the Roman Empire.* Oxford, 1969.

———. "Greek Intellectuals and the Imperial Cult in the Second Century A.D." In *Le culte des souverains,* Entretiens sur l'Antiquité Classique 19, pp. 179–212. Geneva, 1973.

———. "Herodotus, Alexander, and Rome." *The American Scholar* 58 (1989), 407–14. [In Italian as "Erodoto, Alessandro, e Roma," with annotations lacking in the English version, *Rivista Storica Italiana* 100 (1988; published 1989), 724–38.]

———. *Martyrdom and Rome.* The Wiles Lectures, Queen's University of Belfast. Forthcoming from Cambridge University Press.

Bowie, E. L. "The Greek Novel." In *Cambridge History of Classical Literature,* vol. 1, pp. 683–99. Cambridge, 1985.

Burridge, R. A. *What Are the Gospels? A Comparison with Graeco-Roman Biography.* Cambridge, 1992.

Calder, W. M. III. "Aeschylus' *Philoctetes.*" *GRBS* 11 (1970), 171–79.

———. "A Reconstruction of Euripides' *Philoctetes.*" In *Greek Numismatics and Archaeology: Essays in Honor of Margaret Thomp-*

son, ed. O. Mørkholm and N. Waggoner, pp. 53–62. Wetteren, 1979.

Chambers, M. H. *Georg Busolt: His Career in Letters*. Mnemosyne Supplement 113. Leiden, 1990.

Chuvin, P. "La date des Éthiopiques d'Héliodore." In *Chronique des derniers païens*, pp. 321–25. Paris, 1990. [This part of Chuvin's work is omitted from the English translation (Cambridge, Mass., 1990).]

Colonna, A. "L'assedio di Nisibis del 350 d.C. e la cronologia di Eliodoro emiseno." *Athenaeum* 38 (1950), 79–87.

Conte, G. B. "Petronius, *Sat.* 141.4." *CQ* 37 (1987), 529–32.

Conti Rossini, C. "Meroe ed Aksum nel romanzo di Eliodoro." *Rivista degli Studi Orientali* 8 (1919/20), 233–39.

Cullmann, O. *Le problème littéraire et historique du roman pseudo-clémentine*. Paris, 1930.

Desideri, P. *Dione di Prusa: Un intellettuale greco nell'impero romano*. Florence, 1978.

Dihle, A. "Serer und Chinesen." In *Antike und Orient*, Supplemente zu den Sitzungsberichte der Heidelberger Akademie der Wissenschaften, Phil.-Hist. Klasse, 2, pp. 201–15. Heidelberg, 1983.

Dodds, Eric. *The Greeks and the Irrational*. Berkeley and Los Angeles, 1951.

Erim, K. T. *Aphrodisias, City of Venus Aphrodite*. New York, 1986.

Fahd, Toufic. *Artémidore d'Éphèse: Le livre des songes*. Institut Français de Damas. Damascus, 1964.

Feeley-Harnik, G. *The Lord's Table: Eucharist and Passover in Early Christianity*. Philadelphia, 1981.

Foucault, M. *Le souci de soi*. Vol. 3 of *Histoire de la sexualité*. Paris, 1984.

Fowden, G. *Empire to Commonwealth: Consequences of Monotheism in Late Antiquity*. Princeton, 1993.

Frei, H. *The Eclipse of Biblical Narrative*. New Haven, 1974.

Freud, S. *The Interpretation of Dreams*. Vol. 4 of *The Standard Edition of the Complete Psychological Works of Sigmund Freud*, ed. J. Strachey. New York, 1958.

Frye, N. *The Secular Scripture: A Study of the Structure of Romance*. Cambridge, Mass., 1976.

Habicht, C. *Die Inschriften des Asklepieions, Altertümer von Perga-mon.* Vol. 8, part 3. Berlin, 1969.

Heintze, W. *Der Clemensroman und seine griechischen Quellen.* Leipzig, 1914.

Henrichs, A. *Die Phoinikika des Lollianos.* Bonn, 1972. [Translated by G. N. Sandy in *Collected Ancient Greek Novels*, ed. B. P. Reardon, pp. 810–12. Berkeley and Los Angeles, 1989.]

Hoffmann, D. *Das spätrömische Bewegungsheer und die Notitia Dignitatum.* Düsseldorf, 1969–70.

Hopkins, K. "Novel Evidence for Roman Slavery." *Past and Present* 138 (1993), 6.

Housman, A. E. "Two Epigrams of Martial." *CR* 15 (1901), 154–55. [Reprinted in *The Classical Papers of A. E. Housman*, ed. J. Diggle and F. R. D. Goodyear, vol. 2, pp. 536–38. Cambridge, 1972.]

———. *The Confines of Criticism: The Cambridge Inaugural 1911.* Ed. J. Carter. Cambridge, 1969.

Jäkel, S., ed. *Power and Spirit.* Annales Universitatis Turkuensis, ser. B, vol. 199. Turku, 1993.

Jones, C. P. *Plutarch and Rome.* Oxford, 1971.

———. *The Roman World of Dio Chrysostom.* Cambridge, Mass., 1978.

———. *Culture and Society in Lucian.* Cambridge, Mass., 1986.

———. "La personnalité de Chariton." In *Le monde du roman grec,* ed. M.-F. Baslez et al., pp. 161–67. Paris, 1992.

———. "Cynisme et sagesse barbare: Le cas de Pérégrinus Proteus." In *Le cynisme ancien et ses prolongements,* ed. M.-O. Goulet-Cazé, pp. 305–17. Paris, 1993.

Kermode, F. *The Genesis of Secrecy: On the Interpretation of Narrative.* Cambridge, Mass., 1979.

Keydell, R. "Zur Datierung der Aethiopica Heliodors." In *Festschrift F. Dölger,* ed. P. Wirth, pp. 345–50. Heidelberg, 1966.

Kirwan, L. "The Decline and Fall of Meroe." *Kush* 8 (1960), 163–73.

Lacombrade, C. "Sur l'auteur et la date des Éthiopiques." *Revue des Études Grecques* 83 (1970), 70–89.

Lane Fox, R. *Pagans and Christians.* New York, 1987.

Lessing, G. E. *Laokoön*. Ed. K. Balser. Berlin, 1982.

Lightfoot, C. S. "Facts and Fiction—The Third Siege of Nisibis (A.D. 350)." *Historia* 37 (1988), 105–25.

Littmann, E. "Äthiopische Inschriften." In *Miscellanea Academica Berolinensia* 2.2, pp. 97–127. Berlin, 1950.

Luzzatto, M. T. *Tragedia greca e cultura ellenistica: L'or. LII di Dione di Prusa*. Bologna, 1983.

MacAlistair, S. "Oneirocriticism and the Ancient Greek Novel." In *The Ancient Novel: Classical Paradigms and Modern Perspectives*, ed. J. Tatum and G. M. Vernazza, p. 68. Hanover, N.H., 1990.

MacMullen, R. "What Difference Did Christianity Make?" *Historia* 35 (1986), 322–43. [Reprinted in *Changes in the Roman Empire: Essays in the Ordinary*, pp. 142–55. Princeton, 1990.]

Marini, N. "Δρᾶμα: Possible denominazione per il romanzo greco d'amore." *Studi Italiani di Filogia Classica*, ser. 3, 9 (1991), 232–43.

Maroth, M. "Le siège de Nisibe en 350 d'après des sources syriennes." *Acta Antiqua Academiae Scientiarum Hungaricae* 27 (1979), 239–45.

Merkle, S. "Telling the True Story of the Trojan War: The Eyewitness Account of Dictys of Crete." In *The Search for the Ancient Novel*, ed. J. Tatum, pp. 183–96. Baltimore, 1994.

Michenaud, G., and J. Dierkens. *Les rêves dans les "Discours sacrés" d'Aelius Aristide, IIe siècle ap. J.-C.: Essai d'analyse psychologique*. Brussels, 1972.

Milani, L. A. *Il mito di Filottete nella letteratura classica e nell'arte figurata*. Florence, 1879.

Millar, F. "The World of the *Golden Ass*." *JRS* 71 (1981), 63–75.

———. *The Roman Near East*. Cambridge, Mass., 1993.

Mollat du Jourdin, M., and J. Desanges. *Les routes millénaires*. Poitiers, 1988.

Momigliano, A. "The Rhetoric of History and the History of Rhetoric: On Hayden White's Tropes." In *Comparative Criticism: A Year Book*, vol. 3, ed. E. S. Shaffer, pp. 259–68. Cambridge, 1981. [Reprinted in *Settimo contributo alla storia degli studi classici e del mondo antico*, pp. 49–59. Rome, 1984.]

———. "Religion in Athens, Rome, and Jerusalem in the First Century B.C." *Annali della Scuola Normale Superiore di Pisa,* ser. 3, 14 (1984), 873–92. [Reprinted in *Ottavo contributo alla storia degli studi classici e del mondo antico* (Rome, 1987), pp. 279–96; in *On Pagans, Jews, and Christians* (Middletown, Conn., 1987), pp. 74–91; Italian translation in *Saggi di storia della religione romana* (Brescia, 1988), pp. 27–43.]

Mommsen, T. *Römische Staatsrecht.* 3d ed. Leipzig, 1887.

Morgan, J. R. "History, Romance, and Realism in the Aithiopika of Heliodorus." *Classical Antiquity* 1 (1982), 221–65.

———. "Lucian's *True Histories* and the *Wonders beyond Thule* of Antonius Diogenes." *CQ* 35 (1985), 475–90.

———. "Make-Believe and Make Believe: The Fictionality of the Greek Novels." In *Lies and Fiction in the Ancient World,* ed. C. Gill and T. P. Wiseman, pp. 175–229. Austin, 1993.

Munro-Hay, S. "MHDYS and Ebana, Kings of Aksum: Some Problems of Dating and Identity." *Azania* 14 (1979), 21–30.

———. "The Ge^cez and Greek Palaeography of the Coinage of Aksum." *Azania* 19 (1984), 136.

———. *The Coinage of Axum.* New Delhi, 1984.

Olson, S. D. "Politics and the Lost Euripidean *Philoctetes.*" *Hesperia* 60 (1991), 269–83.

Pack, R. "On Artemidorus and His Arabic Translator." *TAPA* 98 (1967), 313–26.

———. "Artemidoriana Graeco-Arabica." *TAPA* 106 (1976), 307–12.

Pelling, C. B. R. "Truth and Fiction in Plutarch's *Lives.*" In *Antonine Literature,* ed. D. A. Russell, pp. 19–52. Oxford, 1990.

Perry, B. E. *The Ancient Romances: A Literary-Historical Account of Their Origins.* Berkeley and Los Angeles, 1967.

Pervo, R. I. *Profit with Delight: The Literary Framework of the Acts of the Apostles.* Philadelphia, 1987.

Pfuhl, E., and H. Möbius. *Die ostgriechischen Grabreliefs.* Vol. 2. Mainz, 1979.

Price, S. R. F. "The Future of Dreams: From Freud to Artemidorus." *Past and Present* 113 (1986), 3–37.

Rankin, H. D. "Eating People Is Right: Petronius 141 and a ΤΟΠΟΣ."
    Hermes 97 (1969), 381–84.

Rattenbury, R. M. "Romance: Traces of Lost Greek Novels." In *New
    Chapters in the History of Greek Literature, Third Series*, ed. J. U.
    Powell, pp. 211–57. Cambridge, 1933.

Reardon, B. P. *The Form of Greek Romance*. Princeton, 1991.

———, ed. *Collected Ancient Greek Novels*. Berkeley and Los Angeles,
    1989.

Reeve, M. D. "Notes on Heliodorus's *Aethiopica*." *CQ* 18 (1968),
    282–87.

Reynolds, J., and R. Tannenbaum. *Jews and Godfearers at Aphrodi-
    sias*. Cambridge, 1987.

Rispoli, G. *Lo spazio del verisimile: Il raconto, la storia, e il mito*.
    Naples, 1988.

Robert, L. *Collection Froehner*. Vol. 1, *Inscriptions grecques*. Paris,
    1936.

———. *Noms indigènes de l'Asie Mineure gréco-romaine*. Paris,
    1963.

———. *Laodicée du Lycos: Le nymphée*. Université Laval, Fouilles.
    Québec and Paris, 1969.

———. "Lucien en son temps." In *À travers l'Asie Mineure*, pp. 393–
    436. Paris, 1980.

Rohde, E. *Der griechische Roman und seine Vorläufer*. 3d ed. Leipzig,
    1914.

Rosenthal, Franz. "From Arabic Books and Manuscripts XII." *JAOS*
    85 (1965), 139–44.

Rostovtzeff, M. I. *Skythien und der Bosporos*. Berlin, 1931.

Ruiz-Montero, C. "Aspects of the Vocabulary of Chariton of Aphro-
    disias." *CQ* 41 (1991), 484–89.

Russell, D. A., ed. *Antonine Literature*. Oxford, 1990.

Rutherford, R. B. *The Meditations of Marcus Aurelius: A Study*. Ox-
    ford, 1989.

Sanday, P. R. *Divine Hunger: Cannibalism as a Cultural System*. Cam-
    bridge, 1986.

Schwartz, E. *Fünf Vorträge über den griechischen Roman*. With an
    introduction by A. Rehm. 2d ed. Berlin, 1943.

Schwartz, J. "Quelques observations sur des romans grecs." *AC* 36 (1967), 536–52.

Smith, Morton. "On the Wine God in Palestine." In *Salo Wittmayer Baron Jubilee Volume,* American Academy for Jewish Research, pp. 815–29. Jerusalem, 1975.

———. *Jesus the Magician.* San Francisco, 1978.

Speidel, M. "Catafractarii Clibanarii and the Rise of the Later Roman Mailed Cavalry." *Epigraphica Anatolica* 4 (1984), 151–56.

Speyer, W. *Bücherfunde in der Glaubenswerbung der Antike.* Hypomnemata 24. Göttingen, 1970.

Stadter, P. A. *Arrian of Nicomedia.* Chapel Hill, 1980.

Straub, J. "Aurelian und die Aksumiten." In *Historia-Augusta-Colloquium 1972/74,* pp. 269–89. Bonn, 1976. [Also in *Quarto congresso internazionale di studi etiopici,* Accademia Nazionale dei Lincei, Quaderno 191, pp. 55–73. Rome, 1974.]

Syme, R. *Ammianus and the Historia Augusta.* Oxford, 1968.

Szepessy, T. "Die Neudatierung des Heliodorus und die Belagerung von Nisibis." *Actes de la XIIᵉ conférence internationale d'études classiques: Eirene,* Cluj-Napoca 1972, pp. 279–87. Budapest, 1975.

———. "Le siège de Nisibe et la chronologie d'Héliodore." *Acta Antiqua Academiae Scientiarum Hungaricae* 24 (1976), 247–76.

Tatum, J., ed. *The Search for the Ancient Novel.* Baltimore, 1994.

Teixidor, J. *Bardesane d'Édesse: La première philosophie syriaque.* Paris, 1992.

Troiani, L. *L'opera storiografica di Filone da Byblos.* Pisa, 1974.

van der Valk, M. "Remarques sur la date des Éthiopiques d'Héliodore." *Mnemosyne* 9 (1941), 97–100.

van Groningen, B. A. *Euphorion.* Amsterdam, 1977.

Vermeule, C. C. "Protesilaos: First to Fall at Troy and Hero in Northern Greece and Beyond." *NM* 38 (1992), 341–46.

Veyne, P. *Did the Greeks Believe in Their Myths?* Trans. P. Wissing. Chicago, 1988.

Visser, M. *The Rituals of Dinner.* New York, 1991.

Winkler, J. *The Constraints of Desire.* New York and London, 1990.

INDEX LOCORUM

GENERAL INDEX

Compositor: Braun-Brumfield, Inc.
Text: 11/14 Sabon
Display: Sabon
Printer: Braun-Brumfield, Inc.
Binder: Braun-Brumfield, Inc.